The
Figure in
Fired Clay

The
Figure in
Fired Clay

A & C Black • London

First published in Great Britain 2001
A & C Black (Publishers) Limited
37 Soho Square
London W1D 3QZ

ISBN 0 7136-5205-5

Cover illustration (front): Egyptian, Badarian figure, ht. 11 cm (4 ¼ in.) d. 4.6 cm (1 ¾ in.), 4500–4000BC. Photograph © The Petrie Museum of Egyptian Archaeology, University College, London (uc.19637, 9601).

Cover illustration (back): Pamela Leung, *Fish Figure Fountain*, 81 x 60 cm (32 x 23 ½ in.). Photograph courtesy of the artist.

Cover illustration (spine): India, Bengal, Tanluk Yakshi or mother goddess, 21.3 cm (8 ½ in.), *c.*200BC.

Frontispiece: Christy Keeney, *Standing Woman*, 37 cm x 10 cm (14 1/2 in. x 4 in.), contemporary. Photograph courtesy of the artist.

Inside cover flap: Photograph of the author © Jonathan Weaver

Cover design by Dorothy Moir
Design by Jo Tapper

Printed and bound in Singapore by
Tien Wah Press Pte. Ltd.

Contents

Persia (Iran), black spout-
ed 'bird', 1300–1100BC
PHOTOGRAPH © ASHMOLEAN
MUSEUM, UNIVERSITY OF
OXFORD

6

Foreword

My subject, the figure in fired clay is a very wide one, and in considering it, the first thing that sprang to mind was a medley of visual images – disparate memories. So images, however random, are the life-blood of this book; and it is on these that any structure, however generalised and imperfect, has been built.

Any close scrutiny of the pictures is likely to be accompanied by a curiosity about the people who made these artefacts and their method of manufacture. Where possible, I have tried to satisfy these questionings by placing each photographed object in a context; in doing so I have gratefully picked the brains of many unsuspecting experts.

But there is one crucial missing element – the actual sense of delight in the handling of clay. Nothing but a small lump of soft clay accompanying these paper pages could have allowed those who have not used it to understand and feel the pleasure of this tolerant, flexible material as well as appreciating the wilfulness of its character. Here there are examples of the immediacy of creation as well as the immense skill of high achievement.

It requires very little for us to identify a figure – either anthropomorphic or zoomorphic. A piece of soft clay with two pierced holes, two gouged slits – one vertical, one horizontal – becomes a face. Thus the gentlest of pressures on the surface of a malleable ball of clay shows us a head; the slightest of bendings, windings and indentations could trigger the idea of a body. Objects and marks are quickly recognised self-referentially; almost anything can look human. Faces and bodies have been represented in an infinite number of ways – from using signs and symbols far removed from reality to photographic verity. Our instincts are such that we can join a child's vision in seeing a dot become an eye, while a chunk of clay can become a goddess or a pot can become a bird. It is this ease of identification that allows quickly modelled clay, however roughly worked, to reach us as an alive, vital image in a way that no other three-dimensional material can.

Figurative sculpture has been and is, perhaps, the most continuous and interesting area of ceramic practice since the dawn of time to the present day.

1
The Earliest Clay Figures

The incoherent world of prehistoric man is hard to imagine. It was a land of forests and monsters, of climatic change, of unpredictable forces of havoc. It needed to be survived but also to be dealt with in a way that was not merely physical. To give form to the incomprehensible hazards was in a sense to control them; to identify these forces with the self helped to make them accessible. To symbolize the successful hunt, for example, was to fulfil 'the human urge to express that which is inherently inexpressible',(Théodule Ribot, 'La Pensée Symbolique') to assuage the terror.

So before the word was the image, and the image was of man himself. The first recorded attempts of man to define the 'real' are pictorial images painted or scratched on the surfaces of rocks and caves, drawings of the victorious hunter and the animals he both feared and needed incorporated into the humps, protruberances and hollows of cave walls. Samples of charcoal taken from cave drawings have been reliably dated as from more than 30,000 years ago, showing that the sophisticated cave art found in such famous caves as those at Lascaux in France and Altamira in Spain existed at a much earlier date than was formerly supposed. While these 'secret' places have been fortuitously preserved, archaeologists also believe that similar Palaeolithic artistic works, now vanished, existed in numerous open-air sites across Europe and beyond. Was it the men who painted scenes of themselves and wild creatures, while the women worked clay into the many fertility figures that are found in so many parts of the world? Without mirrors or pictures they had only their own bodies and how they perceived them to observe and copy when fabricating, as best they could, the objects of intercession which could plead or celebrate their most womanly functions. It has even been suggested that the angle in which many statuettes were formed was that of a female looking downward at herself. Although it is not clearly established who actually was the maker, man or woman, it is assumed that the images of the goddess or fertility symbol fulfilled a common need and were, after all, produced by and for individual women.

One of the most famous figures of the stone age is a limestone carving of a voluptuous woman with pendulous breasts, wide hips, fleshy stomach, generous

Opposite:
Egyptian female torso,
6.6 cm (2 ¼ in.)
3500–3300BC
PHOTOGRAPH © THE PETRIE
MUSEUM OF EGYPTIAN
ARCHEAOLOGY, UNIVERSITY
COLLEGE, LONDON

thighs and small feet. She has no face but it is believed that her elaborate hair-style was symbolic of the mature and fertile woman. She is thought to be 25,000–30,000 years old, and was found near Vienna, Austria, in 1908. Grossly curvaceous and highly fecund, the Venus of Willendorf is quite unlike any classical Venus. Was this an erotic Stone Age fantasy object, a talismatic fertility symbol, an ideal woman for child-bearing or a pregnant woman? But these are limited questions. The archaeologist Richard Rudgely tells us that 'any crude explanation of the Willendorf figurine as simply a fertility figure or an object of desire is entirely inadequate'; rather, that 'the female body was a symbol of cosmological significance that was able to express all aspects of Palaeolithic concerns'; so nothing can be taken at face value – clothing, hair-style, personal adornments such as bracelets can all have symbolic meaning. The Venus of Willendorf was covered in red ochre when she was found, and as this had a widespread function in the Palaeolithic context, it indicated that very likely she was a ritual object.

Like the cave paintings, the Venus figures were made as an appropriate and often individual process by which real people negotiated the physical, social, and spiritual dangers and challenges of everyday life. Woman was not only the biological source of life, of fertility and renewal of life and death, but she was also symbolic, later in Neolithic time, of the agricultural cycle of the year, and a metaphor that encompassed a diverse range of meanings and uses. The approach to image-making tens of thousands of years ago was a practical one in which aesthetic considerations played little part, as between art and technology there was no distinction. While the images might incidentally be objects of beauty they were primarily made to secure by magical means the survival of the race as well as to carry symbolic and social meanings within the culture.

This Palaeolithic Venus (right) was made of limestone and others were made of the same or from horn and mammoth ivory. Were there some from that time made of unfired clay and, like the open-sited paintings, lost forever? When exactly were the thumbed and modelled images made permanent, and where were the earliest fired figures found?

The art of firing clay vessels – pottery – was one of the most important innovations of the Neolithic period, which began about 10,000 years ago. The earliest known ceramic ware has been found in Japan and Siberia. An amazing discovery in 1960 of pots belonging to the Jomon culture, in Japan – the earliest dated 12,500BC – was a surprise even to the archaeologists. To find such an advanced tradition among people whose economy was pre-farming and who therefore seemed to exist in 'primitive' circumstances was unexpected enough, but perhaps even more contrary to general thinking was the discovery that Japan was not dependent on China for ceramic information as was always believed – the earliest known pottery from China has been dated 10,000BC.

Yet this is not the earliest evidence of the existence of ceramic technology, for the making of pots was preceded by an earlier tradition. The deliberate fire-hardening of clay objects has been reported from various parts of the world, not only

Japan and Siberia, but also Russia, North Africa, and the Pyrenees. The earliest of all comes from Moravia in the Czech Republic. In the best known – Dolni Vestonice and neighbouring sites – ceramic artefacts 26,000 years old have been found; these consist of fragments, over half of them pieces of broken animal, and a few human figures. If it is true, as has been suggested, that the making and almost immediate destruction of the figure was deliberate and had some ritualistic meaning, we are left with a strong example where the purely practical was subordinated to some other over-riding purpose.

It is in fired clay that we find many of the earliest forms of sculpture, essentially of women – of young, shapely, nubile women, of pregnant women, of women giving birth, women cradling babies, of earth goddesses, female deities and of women created as votive offerings to deities. Some of the earliest were found in the Indus Valley in Mesopotamia and the neighbouring countries of Egypt, Syria, Cyprus, Crete, Iran and Greece, but similar talismans are found in India, Africa, Mesoamerica, Pakistan – they are universal. Some cultures have been known for some time; others, as we have seen, have been discovered in very recent excavations. For example, a realistic torso of a naked woman in clay, assumed to be part of a fertility cult, was found in China as recently as 1982 and dated c.3500BC. Other timeless figures are still being made: throughout India clay images of the mother goddess are being created today just as they were 4000 years ago. Radio-carbon dating, thermoluminescence and the nature of clay have made it possible to make a relatively accurate dating of these remarkable objects.

While science can alert us to the approximate date of objects it is almost impossible for our imaginations to grasp the idea of the millennia that existed before the birth of Christ. We can usually extend our own historical experience to encompass our own century and a little beyond, but it is difficult to appreciate how miniscule a period it occupies in the sweep of recorded and unrecorded ages, for prehistory occupies an astonishing 95% of our time on this planet. There is a natural tendency to group and name similar objects as though they existed simultaneously in space and time and were of equal significance to their makers. Yet these figures are found across a huge geographical area and over many thousands of years; it is unlikely that they would symbolise the same things to their diverse makers. While anthropologists and archaeologists struggle to make social sense of figurines and have to abide by the uncertainties of historical context, we find that they are often loosely called Venuses, fertility figures, goddesses and earth mothers and we tend to endow them with our own contemporary stereotypical characteristics.

These very early figures are small, the largest is no more than 26 cm (10 ¼ in.) high for they are essentially personal, portable art. Like other small works they are often represented in highly dramatic photographs unrelated to other objects; thus a small terracotta may share the same sense of grandeur as, say, a monolithic Easter Island stone carving. For example, the pre-dynastic Egyptian figure on p.8, with the fan-like tattoo on its back, appears monumental but is actually only 6.6 cm (2 ½ in.) high. Not only are we deluded as to the real scale but our experience is diminished because we are not able to hold it in the palm of our hand to feel the weight, the round volumes and the texture, or to study the markings and gestures on the surface. Nevertheless the printed image can be highly inspirational.

The following illustrations are from much later than the Venus figures of the Upper Palaeolithic period – around 25,000 years ago – and it has been possible to put them into some kind of contextual framework. They illustrate some of the variety of this genre, the seeming universality of intent, the similarity of scale and the originality of the creators of these ancient artefacts.

The figure below – dated somewhere between 3850–3250BC – has something in common with the Venus of Willendorf although, in spite of her great age, she is much younger. The modelling in soft marl clay is far cruder than the more

Egyptian, seated smiling woman, 17cm (6 ¾ in.), 3850–3250BC

Egyptian, Badarian figure,
ht. 11 cm (4 ¼ in.)
d. 4.6 cm (1 ¾ in.),
4500–4000BC

Opposite:
Egyptian, Naquada male
figure, 21.3 cm (8¼ in.)
3500–3000BC

painstaking carving on stone and there is less detail, but the same mature wom-anly bulk – the fullness of breasts and the huge thighs and knees closely relate her to fertility. She is described as a seated, smiling woman although her smile is surely enhanced by erosion. There are very faint tattoo marks on her face and it is thought that this may have been some form of writing which cannot now be deciphered. The seated female figure is a common image in the entire Near East and because of the posture is often interpreted as a woman giving birth. Many of these small statues are funerary figures: this one was found in a grave in Egypt where baked-clay female figures were placed as part of a ritual associated with leading deities, or maybe it was one of the objects and treasures, also found in Egyptian tombs, put there to ensure that the comforts of an earthly existence would be secured in eternity – a concu-bine of the dead.

The delicate figure (left) dated 4500–4000BC is one of the earliest three-dimensional figures from the Nile Valley, and is a good example of the Egyptian ideal of feminine beauty. This young Baderian woman, with wide shoulders, tapering waist and curving hips, has an hour-glass figure. The pubic triangle is represented by an incised line over the belly and over the top of the legs; in the back view an incision separates the protruding buttocks. There is a balance between the exaggerated posterior and thighs and the upper part of the body. The crossed arms have been modelled and joined at the shoulder and elbows.

She has been made from alluvial Nile silt, an homogeneous and consistent material often tempered with straw, ash, dung, or sand; it fires red-black and in this case has been further enriched by a wash of ochre. The nature of this clay gave rise to beautiful, exceptionally thin-walled pots and accounts for the fine finish and delicate modelling of this undecorated form.

There was a virtual absence of the male figure in Neolithic times; when they do appear they are overshadowed by the powerful figure of the goddess.

In Early Dynastic Egypt male figures were often shaped like pegs or blunt nails and were placed in the foundations of temples to ensure divine approval. The male figure (right), with its pointed and bearded chin, has discs of clay for hair. Apart from the modelled penis sheaf the body is unadorned and, indeed, peg-shaped.

Half sitting, half reclining in her tripod-legged throne is the strange figure overleaf. It is dated c.1300–1200BC, an era when the Myceneans, living on mainland Greece, formed a powerful empire which ruled the seas; it traded with Egypt and the Levant for three centuries before being overthrown and extinguished in the 12th century BC.

Throned figures were widely regarded as deities and subjects of religious devotion, and are mainly considered to be votive gifts or grave goods. At least 28 such figures have been found.

Arms outstretched on the high-backed, semi-circular throne, this goddess curiously combines two and three dimensions by painting and modelling. As the

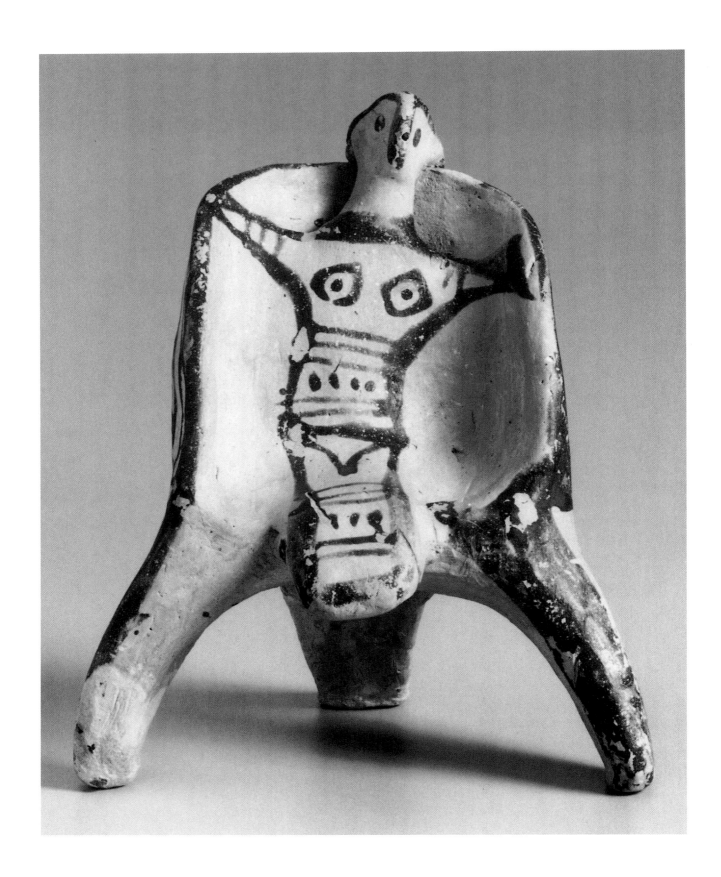

throne tilts back, the body, continuous with the surface of the back-rest, is brought into light relief at the shoulders, while the head is more fully modelled. In addition to the painted features, the red-iron painting on the figure details the stylised pattern on the clothes by rows of dots banded by stripes, while the two-dimensional breasts and pubic area are incorporated into this patterning. The back of the curved throne is also decorated with wavy lines within the outline of the seat. The legs, jutting out from the trough-like seat, modelled and enveloped in cloth, are a particularly unusual feature. Other similar throned deities from this group have separate embryonic legs; in one case they are so inconclusive that they resemble a fish-tail. There is an innocent freshness in the child-like and original representation of this goddess.

The goddess (right) is seated, slim, neat and straight-backed. She is small-waisted, with two small domes of clay for her breasts, and her shoulders slope like a coat-hanger. Her bent legs have been incised from the roll of clay from which she was formed and from which her feet have been pinched out. Her head, continuous with her neck, has a pinched ridge for a nose and indentations for eyes. Coils of clay hang as hair on either side of her face. She too is an enthroned goddess whose throne has not survived, with broken arms which would have extended along the arms of her throne. This solid figure, of red buff clay and decorated with dark brown lustrous glaze, was made in the 8th century BC in Attica – one of the important centres of production in Greece. A very similar figure, static and statuesque, in the Metropolitan Museum in New York, is thought to be a copy and offers evidence of monumental sculpture in the 8th century BC. Others have been found in a funerary context.

The ample form of the figure (overleaf, left) from Syria is dated 5500BC. Although the posture of hands to breast is one of the accepted ways in which to show mourning, her squatting pose – originally on a low stool – is more suggestive of childbirth relating to her fertility. Apart from her head and arms she is modelled in a naturalistic way; her one remaining leg, with the big knee, tapers into a stump with no indication of ankles or feet. The head is merged with the neck,

Opposite:
Greek, Mycenaean, seated throned figure, 9.2 cm (3 ⅝ in.), 1300–1200BC
PHOTOGRAPH © STAATLICHE MUSEEN KASSEL

Greek, Attica, Seated Goddess, 18 cm (7 in.), 8th century BC
PHOTOGRAPH © ASHMOLEAN MUSEUM, UNIVERSITY OF OXFORD

Left:
Syria, Chagar Bazar,
fertility figure, 10 cm
(4 in.), *c.*5500BC

Right:
Cyprus, plank figure,
26 cm (10 ¼ in.),
2300–1650BC

and the somewhat beaked face has been pinched out of the clay; a painted dot representing the eye is placed in the hollow formed by the squeezing of the clay. The figure is decorated with well-placed red lines around the eyes, the neck and across the breast and upper arms; aesthetically satisfying, they would have had cultural significance. This type of figure has been found in Crete and elsewhere in Greece and it also features in the early culture of the Middle Nile.

The strange, flat, stylised figure (*opposite*) of 2300–1650BC comes from Cyprus – a civilisation where the human form appeared in the art of the earliest inhabitants and continued throughout antiquity. In the early Bronze Age it was these plank-shaped terracotta figures which predominated; many were found in tombs. They are recognised as being fertility charms or fertility goddesses.

In such cases our conditioned response allows us to recognise two rectangles as a human figure, the smaller on top and continuous with the larger, even though the modelling is minimal, frequently restricted to a curved handle-like nose, ears and small marble-like breasts. Sometimes they have two or even three rectangular heads and sometimes they carry babies. When they are maternal figures the baby protrudes from the flattened figure – two dimensions turn into three dimensions. The modelled child is a simple shape, for it is stiffly swaddled and lies on an open-hooded cradle board.

They are made from white or red polished clay enlivened by incised or painted decoration. On the white clay the horizontal painted patterning is iron-red, whereas the incised patterns on the red clay are filled with a gypsum paste, which gives a dramatic contrast to the graphic marks indicating headbands, necklaces, belts and facial features. The spontaneity of the decoration is in character with the irregularities of their forming.

Similar figures were also being produced in southern Anatolia at the time and maybe the idea, new and foreign, was thus introduced into Cyprus, for its geographical position was open to influences from many sources.

The decorative technique of incised lines was also found in the contemporary pottery of Cyprus. More organic and more rhythmically patterned, this double-spouted gourd-shaped jug of 2100–2000BC has something of the freedom in making and marking with the plank figure – the beak-like lugs, the eye-like holes – one could almost believe that these two objects were made by the same hand.

Cyprus, double spouted pot, 24.5 cm (9 ¾ in.), 2100–2000BC
PHOTOGRAPH © THE BRITISH MUSEUM

Cyprus, idol, 160 cm
(83 in.), c.2000BC

PHOTOGRAPH BY CHUZEVILLE,
© COPYRIGHT RMN, PARIS

Derived from the more angular and geometric plank figure (*see p.18*), this figure (*left*) is a more human and softer expression of a mother and child. The squared shoulders are now gently formed from the widening neck and the details are carefully modelled. The browed eyes and the ears are precisely pierced, the unbridged nose is pointed and the child, head turned away from its mother, has a face with similar features; the creases of the swaddling are evident and the structure of the board cradle is explicit. The head and neck are continuous, defined by the only decoration, the directly incised marks. The posture and the positioning of the arms clutching the child and the small breasts are similar to those of the plank figure, but the three-dimensional problem of flat slab and modelled figure has been successfully resolved. There is something of the proud parent and watchful animal about this alert and moving figure of the Early Bronze Age.

In the Late Bronze Age the plank figures of Cyprus gave way to female figures in a quite different style – a local adaptation of Syrian sculptures. Unlike the flat plank shapes they are curvaceous and overtly feminine. This figure (*right*) belongs to one such group. Like the Syrian figure, the face is continuous with the head and shaped by pinching out the clay, thus forming a beaked nose without a bridge, jutting straight out from the forehead. On either side of this 'beak' are modelled eyes – studs surrounded by a coil of clay. A notable feature of this group of figures is the large flanged ears which form a curve above the forehead and down to the chin, each pierced with two or three holes which have been found adorned with big circular clay earrings. Typically, they cradle babies in their arms which are always held on the left side of the chest, near to the mother's heart. In this 13th century BC example, with the broken ears, the rudimentary form of the baby may be suckling at the breast. This mother is exceptionally short from the neck to the pubic triangle, which, like the neckband, is roughly marked by incisions. The legs taper into small feet and as in all the other figures we have seen, it is not made to stand up but is an amulet to be held or placed lying down – like a personal 'good luck charm', worn to increase the chances of giving birth. They are often descibed as the Astarte type of figurine, taking the name of the eastern mother goddess.

Cyprus, Enkomi, earring figure, *c*.1450–1200BC
Photograph ©
Ashmolean Museum,
University of
Oxford

21

Another group from Cyprus, such as the figure on the left, is of the same period and also connected to Astarte, the divinity of fertility, was of figures with wide flattened heads who rarely carried babies. Demurely they hold their hands below their breasts, indicating perhaps that they have a different function from that of the last figure. As the posture of hands to breast was a mourning gesture it is usually thought that these were mourning figures placed in tombs as substitute female companions. Desmond Morris has pointed out that they are all shown with feet pointing down as though they were lying on their backs.

In comparison to the previous image this one is much less stylised. Although the eyes have been treated in the same way, the other features are more natural; the nose is sharper and more defined, there is a slit for a mouth, and a chin separates the face from the thick neck. The ears, separate from the head, point down. The breasts are small and pointed, and the pubic triangle, which is like a bikini bottom, is neatly incised, with the diagonal pattern used to represent pubic hair within it. The feet and hands also carry incision marks and the navel is very deliberately pierced. Red and black paint has been used to rim the top of the head, the drawn eyebrows, the neckband and the pubic area.

The baked clay statuette (*right*) from north west Persia (Iran) of 1200–1000BC is remarkable for the simple abstract quality of the form. The continuous outline shape from the softly rounded hairpiece to the waist resembles some sort of spade-like tool. From the topmost point the long shoulderless form gradually widens, then suddenly flairs extravagantly to the magnificent fleshy haunches whose great bulge curves more gently downward to the tiny feet. The rounded ball of the featureless head aesthetically balances the form. The tiny, bent rolled clay arms, symmetrically placed, arrest beautifully

Cyprus, Nicosia, naked woman, 20.4 cm (8 in.), *c.*1400–1200BC

the verticality of the outline. The small stud-like breasts are the only modelled additions to what is an object of instinctive balance and proportion. It is reminiscent of some modern sculpture, for example, Brancusi's bronze *Maiastra* of 1911, the fabulous bird from Rumanian mythology, where the substantial ovalled body is surmounted by the long narrowing neck and a balancing taper to the base. Indeed,it is known that Brancusi was influenced by the origins of art before classical antiquity.

It was probably in the Indus Valley civilisation that the cult of the mother goddess was established, doubtless the amalgamation of many others. The small images were produced in their thousands and the terracotta tradition is a continuous one, for some are still being made today just as they were 4000 years ago. There is a constancy in the simplicity, crudity even, of their making in relation to the sophistication achieved in the working skills of other media. Style and the degree of detail may change but there is little evidence of technical or intellectual progress. It is thought that this was, and is, deliberate, for these images were temporary and disposable although their religious importance was immeasurable.

The figure *(overleaf)* is from Pakistan, *c.*200BC–AD200. It has been quickly modelled from one piece of clay with the nose pinched out. Other features were added, eyes and mouth are pellets of clay squashed and split, the breasts are pierced balls of clay and the navel is a decorated stud. The ornaments, impressed earrings, necklaces and shoulder decorations are also additions. The head-dress, part of the original shape, is enlivened with coils of clay and an impressed headband. In contrast to the schematic character of the front, the back of the figure is voluptuous and naturalistic. Variants of such objects are still being made as toys in present-day Bengal.

North west.Persia (Iran), possibly Amlash, 19.7 cm (7 ¾ in.), 1200–1000BC

North west Province,
Pakistan, 15.8 cm
(16 ¼ in.), *c.*200BC–AD200

Another, of distinctly Indian type, is the small upright plaque bearing a single moulded figure. They have been found at many sites in Northen India from the north-west to Bengal. The plaque illustrated here is from Tamluk in Bengal, at the entrance to the Ganges, and is dated 200BC. It is an exceptionally good example with well-defined detail impressed on a fine red clay. The ornate dress has features in common with other such pieces, the huge head-dress, the large bolster-like earrings which rest on the shoulders and droop over them like epaulettes, the many embossed, hollow bracelets and the rosetted, low-slung girdle. This figure would have been impressed from a stamp or shallow mould, probably itself made of clay, with additions such as impressed rosettes in the background and the combed incisions of the drapery.

India, Bengal, Tanluk Yakshi or mother goddess, 21.3cm (8 ½ in.), *c.*200BC. PHOTOGRAPH © ASHMOLEAN MUSEUM, UNIVERSITY OF OXFORD

These figures have been identified as Yakshis or mother goddesses. At the simplest, a Yakshi is a woman wearing the finery of a royal or high-born lady; but they also represent goddesses created to celebrate the abundance of life, where plants, flowers and body ornaments are commonly used to symbolise the fertility of the earth and its vegetation. The cult of the mother goddess was also widespread and her popular veneration may account for the large numbers of these plaques which have been found.

The figure emerges naturally from the almost barbaric yet delicate ornamentation of the richly modulated texture. The concept of earth and its abundance fashioned into female form is embodied in this clay tablet.

2
The Figure Painted on Clay

As we have seen, the painted figures in the caves pre-dated figures in the round; later still came pots. Figurative elements appear on plates, bowls, and pots and many techniques are used in their drawing – brushwork, incision, *sgraffito*, resist, slip trailing, maiolica, and modelling. The flatness of a plate, the curve of a bowl and the roundness of a pot all pose compositional problems different from those of working on a flat surface of paper or canvas. Ideally there has to be a compromise between the illusory spatial element of a drawing and the real three-dimensional changes of the ceramic piece.

Opposite: Turkey, Phrygia, part of a funerary urn, 32 cm (12 ½ in.), 5th–4th century BC
PHOTOGRAPH © ASHMOLEAN MUSEUM, UNIVERSITY OF OXFORD

This fragment of a funerary urn *(left)* from Phrygia in Turkey, dated to the 5th or 4th century BC, is a flattened form, so the painting in iron on a white slip background is not so dissimilar from working on a flat surface. It shows a seated figure on a horse successfully hunting a deer; apart from the hunter's body all three are in profile – it is a scene of action and success. Like many of the cave paintings it has a vigour and a strong sense of spatial awareness. There is a realism in the observation and an understanding of the excitement of the chase and the energy of a galloping horse.

The beautiful Neolithic droop-mouthed pot *(right)* is from Gansu Province in China, dated 2000–1500BC. It has a full rounded body to which the figures on it have been added in such a way that the man leans stiffly to follow the silhouette of the closing curve of the pot. Shown from the front view the limbs are rendered as angular sticks, and the main body, two triangles with a blob for the head, reduce the whole to a geometric pattern. The nondescript animal is in side view; both the figures are blocked in. The artist has resorted to telling his story, which is perhaps the imperative one of man against beast, in the manner of a pictogram.

China, Gansu Province, ht. 18 cm (7 in.), w. 15 cm (6 in.), 2000–1500BC
PHOTOGRAPH © THE BRITISH MUSEUM

Painted decoration was found on pre-dynastic Egyptian pots and continued until Coptic times (30 BC–AD 641). The earliest pots are the only pictorial record of the time, so are of particular importance, and a lot of attention has been paid to the motifs on them. They show how people lived, their deities and how they worshipped and sometimes narrated historical events. The arrangements of the elements follow a common form and the iconography would have been understood. The Nile occupies the central ground and on it there are oar-propelled or sail-driven riverboats; above and below the river are banks with marsh birds and trees, while human figures are shown hunting, fighting or ambiguously worshipping or watching dancing girls. Often flights of birds in 'S'-shaped formations fly across the space.

In this pre-dynastic squat jar of 3500BC (*left*), we see the reed boat with many oars dipping into the water; on the boat there are two cabins and a standard in the shape of a harpoon. On the far bank a man is hunting, perhaps an antelope, with a boomerang, and on the other side of the river there is an ostrich-like creature and a flight of birds. Each drawing occupies its own space, there is no overlapping and no perspective, each element is represented as though it is in the foreground.

Pre-dynastic pots were either washed with water and pigment or covered with a fine slip of light-coloured clay to lighten them. At this period they were monochromatic, although later polychromatic decoration became common when the pigments used were mineral colours, red and yellow ochre, soot, calcium and cobalt. The pots, of marl clay, were made with such care that it is difficult to say how they were formed, but they were probably coil-built with the slow wheel, in current use, possibly forming the rim.

In the prosperous years of the 7th and 6th centuries BC a school of vase painters arose in Cyprus who specialised in representational designs. Their distinctive style consisted of a single bold design placed in isolation on an otherwise empty ground. This 'free field' pictorial form was characteristic of Southern and Eastern Cyprus. Unsurprisingly, birds were the most popular theme, as Cyprus was host to great numbers on the migration routes between Europe, Africa and Asia. Other subjects were bulls, gazelles, horses, warriors on foot, mounted in their chariots and on ships.

The decoration on this bichrome jug (*right*) shows an aquatic-looking bird hovering in mid-air while its long beak searches out the honey from a lotus blossom; both exist freely in space – there is no ground line. The upper part of the jug has a different life, unrelated to the flat pictorial image. Above the ringed neck, a painted band is interrupted by a dot in a circle (an eye) which

Cyprus, 'free field' painted pot, 18.5 cm (7 ¼ in.), 7th–6th century BC
PHOTOGRAPH © ASHMOLEAN MUSEUM, UNIVERSITY OF OXFORD

29

relates to the spout (a beak). The eye and beak combine with the full volume of the body so that the three-dimensional characteristics of the jug have themselves become a bird.

A larger vessel (*left*), a barrel jug of the same period combines intricate geometric pattern with representational drawings of gazelles and birds. This combination boldly presented on an undifferentiated surface is a more elaborate example of the 'free field' style.

Strong patterning of a representational kind is found on this pre-classic pot from Veraguas in Panama (*below*) dated AD1000–1500, producing a stylised figure from an abstract and symmetrical design. The positive volume of the pot and the flat dimension of the image have been integrated in a powerful way so that the qualities of both are equally poised – distinct and belonging. This is partly achieved by the banding which, placed at the widening and narrowing of the full body including neck and rim, emphasises the circularity of the pot. Between the

Opposite:
Cyprus, 'free field' painted pot, 30 cm (11 ¾ in.), 7th–6th century BC
PHOTOGRAPH © ASHMOLEAN MUSEUM, UNIVERSITY OF OXFORD .

Below:
Panama, Veraguas, pot, 25.4 cm (10 in.), AD1000–1500
PHOTOGRAPH BY CARMELO GUADAGNO, COURTESY OF: NATIONAL MUSEUM OF THE AMERICAN INDIAN, SMITHSONIAN INSTITUTION, N31240.

banding, in the fullest part of the body, is a generous panel for the painting of the crocodile god. By studying the black areas one can see how well balanced are the positive and negative spaces, such as those around the small rounded shoulders, the tassels of the many fingered hands, the spade shape which lies between the legs or the jigsaw puzzle-like piece around the nostrils. The static calm of the clay pot combined with the curves and swirls around the god add to the poised energy of this culturally important mythic figure.

In Greece, figures began to be included in the geometric strips which densely ornamented vases in the early 8th century BC. Stylised representations of men, gods, and animals were occasionally interspersed with a variety of key and chequer patterns, Vs, and zigzags, and are easily overlooked in the continuous frieze patterns which covered the vessels. Some were found marking graves in an Athens cemetary – big funeral urns some five feet tall (16.5 m)– even in the small pitcher (*left*) the figure band shows the dead laid out on a bier with mourners on either side. Narrative scenes, including heroics from popular Greek myths, became increasingly common; as so often happens with pottery remains they are able to give information about things which are unrecorded or which have simply vanished. The extensive survival of Greek pottery, for example, gives some indication of the style and subject matter of the large murals that once covered painted monuments no longer in existence.

Greece, Athens, geometric pitcher, 44.3 cm (17 ½ in.), 730–720BC

In Corinth the direct painting was replaced by a technique in which the figure was painted in black and incised to show the clay colour beneath. The 'red figure' style invented in Athens in 530BC was the exact reverse. The background was painted black, while the figure remained the colour of the clay; light anatomical details were painted with the more subtle implement of a brush, as in the red figure illustrated (*right*).

It was painted on a shallow cup 12.8 cm (5 in.) in diameter, *c*.500BC. A boy carries a covered plate of food in one hand and rolls a hoop along with the other. Within the narrow clay circle enclosed by the wide black border this young man spins his hoop. The rim of the cup, the circle containing the figure and the

off-centre hoop not only echo each other but create a sense of circular motion. At no point does the inner picture touch the border which frames it. The well-expressed feet are placed near the curve of the border in such a way as to suggest that the edge under them is revolving and that he is running as though on a treadmill. Typical of the drawing of this time, the head and legs are in profile while the chest and shoulders are seen from the front. This is a masterly composition: the figure occupies the whole ground designated for it vertically and in the horizontal plane the left arm extends to the edge while the right arm holding the stick and the bent head parallel the inner circle.

The shallow circular field designated for the decoration of this Greek cup lends itself to a graphic linear design with no scope for variety of tone, while the dark background forces the figure into the foreground. It is suitable for a single figure study such as this, an image which could be enjoyed by the drinker as he sups his wine.

Italy, Chiusi, boy with a hoop, 19.6 cm (7 ¾ in.), *c.* 500BC

PHOTOGRAPH © ASHMOLEAN MUSEUM, UNIVERSITY OF OXFORD

A bowl from the Garrus region of Northeast Persia, 10th–13th century AD, makes an interesting compositional comparison with the previous Attic cup in the way the figure has adapted to its circular boundary *(see below)*. Here the human-headed beast claws its way round its confines, with head cast back, in its own active, never-ending motion. In this type of bowl the central medallion is usually occupied by a human or animal figure, and in addition the well and the rim are decorated with patterns which make maximum use of *sgraffito*. This is a technique where a vessel is covered with a slip which is scratched or cut through

Persia, Garrus area, bowl, 16.1 cm (6 ⅜ in.), 10th–13th century AD

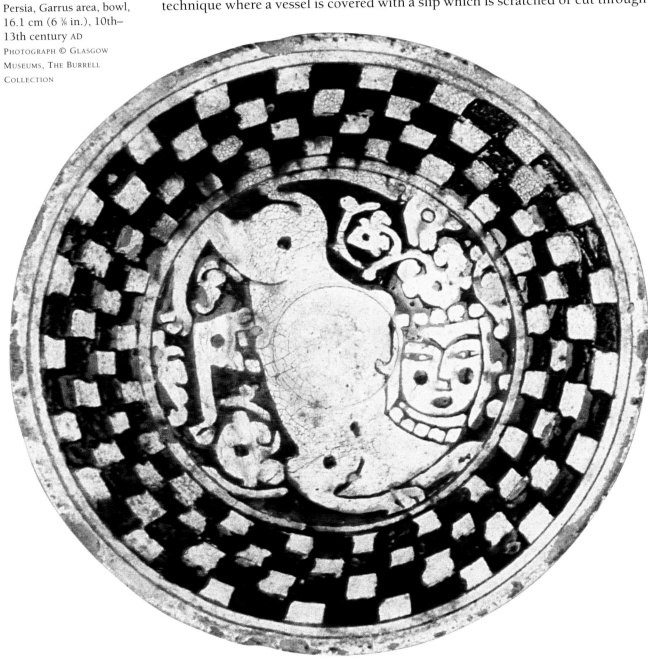

to expose the different coloured body underneath. Here the dark body has been covered with a pale slip, producing a contrast that may have been heightened by painting the darker areas with a brown pigment. This is the first glazed vessel in this chapter and in this example a clear glaze has been used.

The bowl below has not only been covered with an opaque, cream glaze but has been further fired with a lustre one. The latter technique – where the pot is painted with a very thin metallic coating and fired for a third time in a low, carefully controlled, reduction atmosphere – was invented by Islamic potters in the 9th century AD in Iraq. It was probably developed for its glittering effect which imitated precious metal.

Persia (Iran), lustre bowl, 20 cm (7 ⅞ in.), AD1211– 12

In the Persian (Iranian) lustre bowl *(right)* the white ground gives scope for all-over ornamentation. Indeed, there is a dense texture of tightly wound spirals painted on the women's dresses and in the background, making a delicate goldenbrown tone from which the pale Buddhist female moon faces shine out as they look into the stream. Unlike the other painted pots we have seen these figures exist in a recognisable environment – a garden with plants, birds and fish. The six women – their halos are marks of distinction – sit close together, skilfully and elegantly fitting into the curved, circular surface of the vessel. Faces, hands, leaves and fish have been painted minimally with the lustre, providing white accents in the refined richness of the overall texture. Lustre, like many other technical discoveries, seems to have been a secret process. The centre for the Persian industry became Kashan where this peaceful and serene bowl comes from, and is dated AD1211–12.

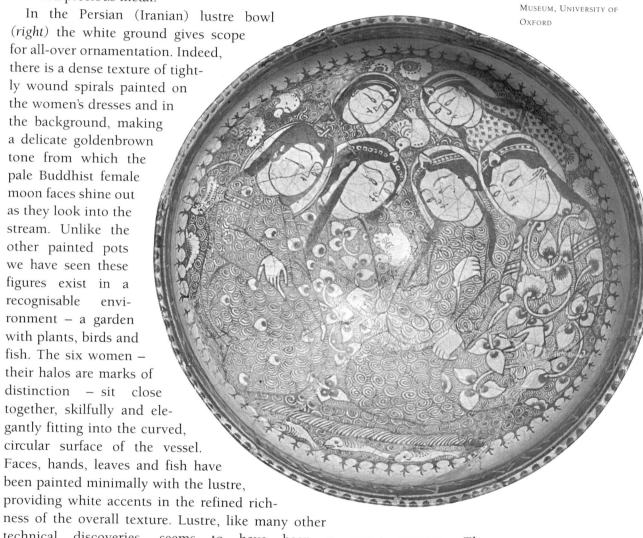

During the Renaissance, shortly before AD1500, the lustre process, gained from the Hispano-Moresque Islamic world, became known in Europe and was

later used to enrich the more universal maiolica ware of the 17th and 18th centuries. The small town of Deruta, south of Perugia, dominated by the maiolica industry since the Middle Ages, adopted it, combining this with their skill in tin-glazed earthenware.

The technique of maiolica involved firing an undecorated dish or vessel to 1000°C/1832°F then dipping it into an opaque white glaze. When the powdery glaze was dry it was painted with oxides and fired again to a slightly lower temperature; the principal colours obtained were blue, green, purple and brown, yellow-orange and white. The lustre was then painted onto the dish and fired for a third time to a lower temperature in a reducing atmosphere.

Italy, Deruta, maiolica dish, 42.4 cm (16 ⅝ in.), 16th century AD

The early 16th century dish of the huntsman blowing his horn (*above*) is from Deruta. The artist uses a very limited palette – the white of the tin glaze, the blue of the outline and the pale gold of the metallic coating. The wide rim of the plate is covered with a scale pattern characteristic of this ware; the lustre picks it out as well as the figure, the castle, and the stylised trees and flowers. The unlustred background indicates the link between the Italian maiolica and that which arose in other parts of Europe known as delftware and faïence.

The scene occupies the concave centre of the plate. Compositionally there is an emphasis on the vertical and the horizontal, the vertical by the uprights of the figure, the three rhythmically patterned trees and the castle turrets, and the horizontal by the disposition of the dogs, the landscape, and the horn and feather. Apart from a slight modelling on the face the painting is flat, and perspective is indicated by the overlapping of forms.

Although there was a skilful control of the ceramic technique, maiolica-decorated plates and vessels were essentially a painter's art, being painted either by known craftsmen or by employed journeymen. The elaborate subject matter, known as *istoriato*, was often copied from woodcuts or engravings. It has been suggested that this scene may reflect a lost 15th-century Florentine engraving.

The technique of maiolica was brought to the Low Countries from Italy in the 16th century and from there to Britain, where it became known as English delftware. As with Italian maiolica painters, pictures were often copied from the work of fine artists.

This image *(below)* painted in London in the mid-17th century came from an engraving which was itself made after a painting and is so boldly and freely

English, London, maiolica dish, 40.6 cm (16 in.), 17th century AD

PHOTOGRAPH © ASHMOLEAN MUSEUM, UNIVERSITY OF OXFORD

drawn that one suspects it is a very casual copy. The unsophisticated drawing found in English delftware, and the relatively few colours used – mainly blue, green, yellow and brown – made for a naive simplicity and child-like charm. The subject matter was largely figurative, and included kings and queens, personalities of the time and biblical subjects. The story of Adam and Eve was a favourite, and in this plate, made in London, they are seen coyly trying to hide their newly discovered nakedness, after the serpent, coiled around the tree of Good and Evil, has persuaded them to eat the forbidden apple.

Large slipware chargers made during the 17th and 18th centuries in Staffordshire in England used similar subjects to those of English delftware – figures, animals, informal portraits and kings and queens. However, their character was completely different; the method of decorating pottery with coloured slips under a transparent glaze did not lend itself to accurate drawing but resulted in highly decorative dishes and a mellow surface. Wet clay added to a leather-hard body produced particular and unique fusions and bleedings. Thomas Toft was the outstanding master of some of the 16 potters working on slipware. First a dish was thrown and turned or, if it was a large oven dish, press-moulded, and a white slip poured over it to cover the red clay. The outline was then trailed in dark slip and later filled in with a buff one; finally white dots might be piped on the outline enlivening the rich decoration. The border of the plate was an excuse for further decoration, often a closely criss-crossed pattern combined with a signature or a commemoration. Once biscuit-fired the pots were glazed and fired to an earthenware temperature.

Mary Wondrausch, an exponent of the slipware technique, is one of the few contemporary potters to have used it with such controlled skill. In this slip-trailed commemorative charger (*right*), she has combined two traditional images, King James I and Queen Elizabeth I, to represent a wedding couple who are named on the border. The dish is covered with a honey glaze which gives the dish a unifying warmth.

All the decorated pots that we have looked at so far were fired at an earthenware temperature, that is below 1100°C/2012°F. The contemporary potter, Eric James Mellon, wanted softer, more muted colours and a less shiny glaze for his figurative decoration, so he needed to fire to a higher, stoneware temperature. To achieve this he had to overcome the problem that the oxides he wished to use were fluxes which would cause his graphic line to distort and bleed. It took many years experimenting with ash glazes before he found an appropriate one that could be fired in excess of 1300°C/2372°F without distorting his drawings.

His self-taught ceramic expertise is combined with graphic skills, particularly in life drawing, which he practises constantly. Sometimes he draws directly from the model onto the clay, but it is mostly his completed drawings, watercolours or monoprints which are the main source of his decoration. Once the figures have been outlined on clay he paints with oxides in much the same way as he would with watercolour paints. He recognises that any decoration – the shapes within the picture – must assist in the perception of the ceramic form, otherwise the

composition might just as well stay on paper or canvas. He writes: 'A bowl is round and most vases are spherical and lines and movements must therefore recognise curves not just straight lines.'

Mellon's work has been described as poetic-figurative. His subjects include the circus, classical mythology and folklore characters such as the moon goddess, mermaid figure and the bird maiden.

This pot of his (*see overleaf*) is one on the theme of tenderness. A clear linear drawing outlines the figures, pale against the brown background of this bulbous

English, Mary Wondrausch, slip-trailed dish, 40 cm (15 ¾ in.), 1996

PHOTOGRAPH COURTESY OF THE ARTIST

English, Eric James Mellon, *Theme of Tenderness* series, stoneware vase, 16 cm (6 ⅜ in.), 1986

pot, 15 cm (6 in.) high. The figures of the lovers and the lions are adapted to this full-bodied form, circling the base and width of the pot and curving over its shoulder. The lion is a recurring motif in Mellon's work, representing a doorway, new life, death and life after death and as a herald of a new-born child. As well as common symbols, there is always added a personal symbolism of subtle, auto-biographical significance.

Eric Mellon is unusual among present day potters in the understanding and emphasis he places on academic composition and drawing and in his use of high-fired stoneware for story-telling to evoke his own magical vision.

Another artist potter working a few years earlier whose interest lay in the female figure, was R.J. Washington. Like Eric Mellon he was a painter with ambitions to be a potter, but his interest lay outside colour; his particular engagement was to integrate sculpture and drawing, to synthesise a painter's feeling for paint with a potter's love of clay. He viewed the profile of the tall stoneware bottles he threw on the wheel – often in two parts luted together – as an extension of drawing. He made tall, thin pots because the great advantage of height was to maximise the variations and changes of the profile enough to invoke the outline of a woman's torso. The quality of this physical line could be compared to that of the painted one. Washington's brushwork moved from the Eastern mark towards cubist-style images, which may have been influenced by Picasso's paintings. The spiky, geometric, mainly female figures painted in red iron oxide extended to the full height of the pot, echoing its gentle curves – transparent forms with bird-like heads drawn on a clay lover's heavily fingered thrown pot.

The highly original potter, Bernard Palissy (1510–90), may have been influenced by the Italian maiolica ceramicists who were commissioned to work in France. He spent 15 tortuous years searching for the 'full perfection of the white enamel', by which he meant the tin glaze used in maiolica – knowledge that was so painfully acquired but not passed on to other potters. Uniquely, Palissy's dishes and plates were not only painted but erupted in relief and modelling. Surfaces were disturbed by snakes, fish, serpents, plants and leaves which twined and writhed over the ornate naturalism of his 'rustic' ware. By the end of the 17th century this curious type of work was no longer made. Little is known of the artist but a revival of Palissy ware in the 19th century acknowledged the style of the innovator.

The earthenware dish (overleaf), from the late 16th century, questionably attributed to Palissy, indicates the elaboration of such press-moulded, relief ware. The detailed picture, 'La Belle Jardinière', is probably a copy of a print. Flora is shown wreathed in flowers, holding a bouquet aloft in one hand and cradling a sheaf in the other, while around her lie garden implements. Below her in the background a man and woman are carrying on their heads produce from the garden, which is laid out in the neat perspective one would expect of a formal French garden belonging to a château or a palace. The rim is embossed with a design after a German silver platter, and has been coloured in imitation of the metal.

Like Bernard Palissy, Pablo Picasso (1881–1973) added three-dimensional features to some of his plates to such an extent that they, too, lost their function as dishes. This towering genius of the 20th century, famous for his painting, sculpture, printmaking and drawing is perhaps less well known for his ceramics.

It was in 1947 that he began to work in clay in the workshop of Suzanne and Georges Ramies in Vallauris in the south of France. The Ramies recalled that in

English, R.J. Washington, *Resurgence*, 90.3 cm (35 ½ in.), 1980
PHOTOGRAPH BY THE ARTIST, COURTESY OF: SU LAPASCO WASHINGTON

1948 over 600 different subjects were illustrated by him on rectangular 32–8 cm (12 ½–15 in.) meat plates. He was 66 years old.

Picasso brought together all that he had learned in a life-time's work in painting, drawing and sculpture, so much of the painted subject matter was inspired by his work in other media, such as fauns, goats, bullfights and still lives.

'My father never considered himself a potter,' wrote Claude Picasso, 'but approached the medium of clay as he would any other in order to find out what materials and techniques of the potter's studio could offer him and what he could discover by pushing their inherent qualities and possibilities.'

He exploited to the full the wonderful plasticity of clay and the inviting surfaces which could be worked in so many ways. He painted, gouged, incised, and modelled surfaces on which he experimented by overlaying glazes, oxide, enamel, slip and wax-resist, all of which would become transformed in the wood-burning kiln. Everything was grist to his mill; there are photographs of him neatly eating his fish lunch, rescuing the clean skeleton and pressing it into the soft clay of a fish-shaped slab which was then luted on a press-moulded dish. The fish with its impressed backbone was now back on his plate. Ideas begat ideas as dishes became faces and bullrings or plates with ceramic meals, as two dimensions played with three dimensions. In one dish a wrist stretches from under the roughly painted stripes of a blue tablecloth, terminating in large, pink three-dimensionally curved fingers. On another, glazed in shiny green, a modelled fish with corrugated scales is ready to be eaten with a fork on one side and a slice of lemon on the other with the tail and head overlapping the round platter.

Above all, faces were constantly painted on plates of different sizes. On rectangular meat dishes, faces filled the whole of the oval bases, allowing the slightly crinkled rims to be decorated with stripes, dots or marks representing hair and beards – some are brilliant and enamelled, others dark, gouged and impressed – with wide faces or long faces according to the direction of the dish. Rimmed and unrimmed round plates provided other surface shapes on which to experiment, sometimes directly painted, while on others faces were built up on impressed grids and corrugations. Interspersed with his three-dimensional ceramics, the first plates were painted in 1947 and Picasso continued to experiment with a vast range of images – in relief, gouging the surface and applying various applications of colour – on plates and tiles until the 1960s.

The oval-rimmed dish above was decorated in 1947. The *Head of a Faun* occupies the base of the plate; a continuous line draws one eyebrow, the nose, the main outline of the head and one cheek, which is scratched into the clay and left largely uncoloured. Similar *sgraffito* marks fill in the ears, horns, moustache and lips and these have been infilled with painting. Round, pierced holes are used for the nostrils, the irises and the texturing of the beard. The striped rim encloses and becomes part of the the head and plays the warm brown of the iron against the cool cobalt and manganese painting, echoing the rich colour of the exposed clay with the dark cool painting of the head.

The many subjects, such as the still life, faces, seated flute players, and fauns are known to us in paintings, and while they also remain familiar to us in clay, we are aware that they have been transformed by the inventions which arise when the expressive possibilities of the ceramic medium itself is creatively explored.

Spanish, Pablo Picasso, *Head of a Faun*, 38 x 32 cm (15 in. x 12 ⅝ in.), 1947, private collection

3
The Pot as Figure

In Chapter Two we found that it was the art of the painter, using the sophisticated skills of accumulated knowledge, that enabled the figure, although on a flat surface, to be depicted in space. In the case of the pot-figure the volume of the pot itself meant that no such complex understanding was necessary, for the vessel already occupied the third dimension and already existed in space. From earliest time the pot – the sense of volume indivisible from the form – has been used to represent the figure in sculptural pieces. The body, the shoulder and the neck of the pot may indeed become the body, shoulder and neck of a human form (*see p.46*), the handle and spout may contribute or even be a carrier of the image (*see p.44*), or these utilitarian chacteristics may be overlooked in the richness of the decoration or modelling (*see p.49*). A pot may be turned upside down and become the base on which a figure is built, or it may become the ground on which a whole group exists (*see p.56*). Figures may sit on the edge of bowls, grow out of them or clamber all over them. Sometimes the whole volume of the vessel becomes the body, while at other times it is the lid that bears the figurative element. Everyday vessels are often adapted by additions but sometimes a figure is made in the anthropomorphic shape it is finally intended to be.

The pot-figure often carries with it symbolic overtones. For example, the formally decorated Athenian pitcher (*see p.32*) has two small nipples modelled on the front; they have no relevance to the painted geometric patterning but were presumably intended to evoke the long held idea of woman as vessel.

The moulded Canopic, Egyptian pots of 15th century BC had lids with human heads modelled on them, and as they were the containers which held parts of the body removed in preparation for burial, they were as important as the coffin – 'the deceased's house' – in rituals and in the idea of preserving the body after death.

Cremation was the universal rite in Etruria in the 8th century BC and the funerary urn was considered not only as an object to protect the dead but, in some way, to represent them. Portrait-like heads were placed as lids on jars, which were themselves sometimes made in simplified human form, implying that the jar was itself the dead.

Opposite:
Central Iraq, Kish, vase with strap handle, 41 cm (16 ¼ in.), 2300BC
PHOTOGRAPH © ASHMOLEAN MUSEUM, UNIVERSITY OF OXFORD

Egypt, black figure vessel,
42 cm (16 ½ in.),
4th century BC
PHOTOGRAPH © ASHMOLEAN
MUSEUM, UNIVERSITY OF OXFORD

Mod ⌐ ⌐n the lid may provide solace in other ways; a ⌐ ⌐ss on the lid of a cinerary urn found in Um ⌐ ⌐ecomes the guardian of the ashes, while the lid on such an urn in Mexico has open-mouthed twins who seem to be praying or singing to higher beings, invoking them to intercede for the departed.

Animals have their own symbolism. A Moche pot from Peru is in the form of an owl – a symbol, among other things, of the spirit of the dead. The head of a sphinx modelled on the mouth of an Islamic ewer expresses its role of a bringer of good luck.

Pot-figures have been made for a variety of reasons. They may be fertility figures, or they may have another cult function (see opposite). They are often used importantly as funerary objects, as the above examples show. They may be luxury items such as the small Egyptian sculptures used for expensive cosmetics, or they may, like some of the Moche pots of Peru, portray daily life (see p.53). More than one purpose may be combined in a pot.

One of the simplest examples of a container taking on the presence of a human figure is the jug (see p.44) from Iraq in the Northern end of the alluvial plain of Mesopotamia; for the 'figure' occupies only the small area of the strap handle of a somewhat coarsely made jug. It is a startling and commanding image delicately modelled. The structuring of the eyes and the small tip-tilted nose and slightly open mouth indicate an awareness of the value of light and shade in expressing the protruberant facial features, while the simple round blobs of the breasts, indicating woman, suggest that this jar is probably associated with a fertility goddess. It is interesting to compare the banal flat, scratched decoration and the fingered coil around the shoulder of the pot with the sophistication of the relief modelling. It was in excavations after World War I that such amazing items of early history were unearthed. This jug, possibly representing the Sumerian goddess Imin, was found in the major historic city of Kish in central Iraq and is dated c.2300BC.

The Egyptian black vessel (above) has been transformed into a figure by the easiest of means. The shape of the pot itself is suggestive of the human form, more particularly of a female form, moving as it does from a small base and broadening out into the wide thighs and hips of a woman, until it arrives at the waist where the neck of the pot suggests the torso, which is completed by the

Nigeria, Edo people,
Benin, figure pot, 34 cm
(13 ½ in.), *c.* 20th century
PHOTOGRAPH © COPYRIGHT THE
BRITISH MUSEUM

open-holed head. The small stump arms have been pulled out from the clay and thumb marks are seen clearly on them and on the ears, the hint of a nose has been squeezed and dragged to the rim of the pot and the carefully formed breasts have probably been added. The emphasis on the wide hips and breasts is the hallmark of the fertility figure which this is conjectured to be. It dates from the 4th century BC and is approximately contemporary with the Egyptian fertility figures in Chapter 1.

In contrast, this pot from Nigeria (*above*) is heavily ornamented and richly modelled. Rather than becoming the pot, the figure is integrated with it so that, while part of each other, pot and figure keep their own identities. The pot will be kept filled with fresh water, for it has come from an Olokun shrine of a woman who belongs to the Edo people of Benin, and is associated with her fertility.

The sculpture is attached to the pot by the neck and head. The fingernailed hands rest on the armchair or throne, while the arms echo the series of handles that are arched around the pot with the feet resting on a specially added ledge. The decoration, direct and positive, is scratched and gouged vigorously into the clay, and includes the scarification marks on the cheeks of the boldly modelled, broad-nosed face with its traditional head-dress. Strips of clay are added for the collar and cuffs, and the pythons which twine around the jar represent messengers of the gods. Clearly, realistic proportions are of no great consideration and even the pregnant condition of the cult devotee is only mildly indicated in what is an expressive object highly significant to the owner. It is the awareness of this ritual importance, combined with the unerring consistency of its making, rather than the formal aesthetic qualities, that make this pot so moving and satisfying. It was probably made in the early part of the 20th century.

In the ceramics of medieval Europe the face-jug was particularly popular. Most domestic ware was plain or undecorated but some more ornate pieces seem to have been intended to amuse or entertain at mealtimes. A human face, often a bearded man, frequently formed the spout, and sometimes the whole jug was made into a human figure by the addition of strips of clay or coils forming thin arms from the shoulders or hands appearing above the stomach. Details of clothing, such as brooches or buttons, anthropomorphised the vessel. There was even greater elaboration in Britain and Europe between AD 1250–1350. An example of this using both animals and men was the 'knight jug' where several modelled figures, with shields and on horseback, were applied to the neck of the jug.

This 14th-century jug (*left*) from Sussex is simpler. A face (partly reconstructed) has been modelled onto the rim while an addition of what appears to be a shield – described as a buckle and rosette – rests on the full, rounded body. Curved flattened strips of clay from the bottom of the neck to just above the base give an energy to the jug's surface. It has been glazed with the recognisable medieval green lead glaze, and although there are no arms there is a feeling that at the other side of the pot the shield is being held very firmly.

The jug has the typical round base of many pots of that time. Bernard Leach, puzzling over this, conjectured that the only practical way they could have been made was by building the pot without a base then 'stitching' one on: the heavily impressed finger marks may be the result of this method.

A moulded jug from Greece (*right*), 15 cm (6 in.) high, is shaped like a woman's head. Attic head vases formed a large category of objects clearly intended for women, such as cosmetic and trinket boxes and perfume jars. However, jugs of this type were frequently made into satyr and

48

Greek, Attic, maenad head
vase, 15 cm (6 in.), 15th
century BC
PHOTOGRAPH © ASHMOLEAN
MUSEUM, UNIVERSITY OF
OXFORD

maenad figures and used for serving and drinking wine. The functional aspect
here is dominated by the visually striking head in much the same way that the
boldly painted features dominate the modelling. The carefully drawn, darkly
filled-in eyes, with the scratched irises, and the outlined lips follow the modelling but appear in front of the unpainted relief of the eyelids and mouth. The
repeated arch of the eyebrows is stylised compared to the naturalism of the modelled features. Yet there is an easy tension between the non-tonal flatness of the

painting and the idealistic realism of the sculpted features. The transition from the light face with its dark markings to the blackness of the upper part of the pot, including the lip and handle, is mediated by the rhythmical dots of the head-dress which frame the face – white blobs with dark centres.

It has been noted by an American art historian, Marilyn McCully, that a significant number of Picasso's jugs and vases which read as sculptural heads hark back to Attic jugs where the anthropomorphic quality, enhanced by painting, derives from the shape of the vessel.

This unusual bell-like idol (*below*) is from Boeotia, Greece. The torso is an upturned stemmed bowl in which the separately modelled legs are suspended. The little coiled arms and the modelled breasts, nose and ears are added and it is painted in much the same schematic style as the vases of the time, (*see p.32*). The wide skirt is circled by a line of dancing women with hands joined; they are interwoven with floral devices made up of dots and circles and unusually a bib hangs between the breasts. The painting is less severely geometric and linear than that on the vase, and although the motifs are symmetrically placed, the surface is more freely explored.

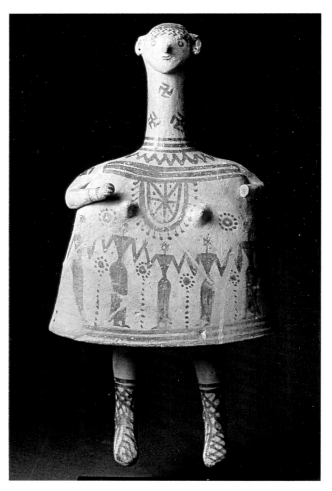

This figure is dated 700BC. Bell-shaped figures with wheel-made bodies, sometimes with detachable legs, were also but infrequently found in 5th century Cyprus.

The twin figures forming the Turkish vase (*right*) have been moulded into their strange asymmetrical form. Although it is a double-necked container it has clearly not been derived from a domestic vessel. It does not stand up, as the round bottom does not balance the upper body, so it was probably placed in a tomb.

The life of the heads arises directly from the way the clay has been treated, from the modelling of the overhanging eyebrows which curve into the beak-like nose and the dark pierced depths of the eyes. The eyes would normally have been filled in with obsidian. The female figures have little coil arms – reminiscent of some medieval pots – which are bent under large flat breasts. The bulge of the common stomach and the exaggerated twin bulges behind, give the pot a rippling silhouette which can be particularly appreciated by following it on the right hand side of this photograph. The painted lines are rhythmical and inventive. This pot is very much in the round – sculptural in its varied view points, vessel-like in its internal volume.

It was originally dated 500BC but was discovered

Turkey, twin figure vase, 500BC (forgery)
PHOTOGRAPH © ASHMOLEAN MUSEUM, UNIVERSITY OF OXFORD

to be a forgery. The unusual cracking of the surface and the pigment which could not be accurately matched to the original mineral alerted experts to its contemporary manufacture. It was actually made in the 1960s following exciting excavations in Turkey the decade before. Nevertheless, it was sufficiently like this type of Neolithic artefact to have been thought genuine.

The Moche people of Peru are known firstly for their ceramics and secondly for their textiles. The earliest pots were made just before the time of Christ while the latest were being made in the 9th century AD. Their portrait pots are unlike anything else found in Andean art for they are remarkably realistic. The early heads were hand-made but later, with the development of mould-making, there was a proliferation of other types of ceramic. There were full figures, figures cast

on top of vessels, painted vessels and combinations of painted vessels with figures on top.

Each of the clay portrait heads (*see above, left*) is a stirrup spout bottle, which
consists of a chamber with a hollow handle and a spout set on top, in the form
of a stirrup. Many heads are known, featuring 50 individual portraits, only one
of which is likely to be a woman. In fact, the only time in the history of
Mesoamerica when female figures outnumbered those of men was when small
hand-made pieces were made in the earliest surviving works of 2500BC.

The position of the stirrup and the placing of the upright head suggests that
this is probably an early hand-made example. The somewhat blurry character of
the features also suggest modelling, rather than the crisper result of moulding.
The wide flaring nostrils indicate a negroid element, and this racial type can be
found nearly everywhere in ancient Mesoamerica, if only in small numbers and
in isolated instances. The pre-Columbian heads reveal that the population was
exposed to intensive and varied intermingling of races.

These pots from North Peru tended to use a two-colour slip decoration of red
and white clay. This example is not decorated by painting, however, but by the
low relief which was often used in preference and seen here on the band of the

52

head-dress, the embossed emblem above and the commonly used stamping.

The charming Moche pot (*opposite*) in the form of two birds is of a later date. Spout and chamber would have been made separately; here the lower part of the chamber may have been moulded four fifths of the way up from a two-piece mould, with the rest coiled and modelled and then luted to the moulded spout by a coil. This joining sometimes causes stirrup pot handles to come away from the body of the pot and there is evidence of a repair at this juncture. A fine white slip, covering and fired on the form, has been painted with a post-firing application of organic black pigment. The entwined birds, their extended wings patterning the body of the pot, are integrated to the handle by the black strip of head and spine rising over the spout. Glazes were not used in pre-Spanish Peru; the body would have been burnished with a hard stone when the pot was nearly dry to give it a glaze-like sheen.

Because of the weakness of the joins these bottles were clearly not very practical, and the most likely explanation for their purpose was as essentially decorative vessels with an aesthetic rather than a utilitarian function.

The Moche art of Peru is essentially narrative, active and full of organic life; it emphasises action – even funerary pottery celebrates the joy of living. Women seem to have occupied a relatively unimportant position in their representation but here there is an example of one with a herculean task (*below*) as she gets

Peru, Moche, woman with large pot, 13 cm (5⅛ in.), Pre-Columbian

ready to lift a large pot. The padded net on her forehead widens as it circles and decorates the vessel and ties her forever to it. As in the Yoruba cult pot the figure is modelled on the container. The body is built from the wall of the pot but the head, fully in the round, occupies its own space and is skilfully modelled with the fine features associated with the Mesoamerican Indian. She wears a loose tunic and, like today's inhabitant of Moche, has bare feet. Compared to the care and beauty of the modelling of the face the arm is surprisingly rubbery, a fat bent coil emerging from the pot. What is in her load? Is it one of the large jars in which chicha, the important maze wine is fermented? And would such a large jar have had a lid, as the two holes near the top suggest?

On the pots below, it is the lid that has been used to transform these cooking pots into women, who themselves are carrying shapes similar to those on which they stand. They are both vessel and carrier so surely the idea of the interchangeability of woman and vessel is inherently stated in these pots for sacrificial offerings. They come from the Yoruba region of Badagri Abuya in Nigeria and share many of the sculpted idioms of the Edo cult pot (see p.47) though the modelling here is more deliberate and skilful, more akin to the refinement of similar wood carvings. The facial features are modelled in relief, the tall hairstyle is well balanced and better proportioned and the scarification marks identify a different group of people. The strap handles, another common feature, are used both to form the figure and to support it, and are edged with neatly placed

Nigeria, Yoruba region, women carrying pots, approx. 15 cm (6 in.), nd

impressed marks. In addition there are carefully formed bosses patterning the handle and the base of the casserole. With their wide skirts, it is with a natural grace that these women grow out of the pot. The photograph was taken *c*.1950, so this is probably a 20th century fabrication.

The figure from Luristan, Persia *(below)*, is a closed form, and is no longer a vessel. In spite of the strange head and the upturned slippers, it is in many ways very close to being a spouted pot. It has been covered with a cream slip and painted with red iron in the same abstract way as the pot being held and is typical of the painted style of pots of the time. The phallus is an adaptation of the handles found on vessels which are placed straight onto the body of a jar, not unlike the common earthenware cooking pots from France or Spain, and is joined to the body in the same way.

Luristan, Persia (Iran), figure holding a vessel, 24 cm (9 ½ in.), *c*.850BC
Photograph © Ashmolean Museum, University of Oxford

Holding a large water jar the celebrant pours a libation, which seems to be an image of an act of respect and worship not necessarily carried out by a holy man. This appears to be a grave ornament and protected underground it has remained complete. In Egypt it is known that special water jars were used to pour libations in the purification ceremonies which were a necessary preliminary to all funerary and temple rituals, so perhaps a similar ceremony is being illustrated here. The figure was found in the mid-20th century and is dated *c.*800–700BC.

It is interesting to compare this image with a pot painted by Picasso based on a traditional Provençal form which has a bulbous spout high on the body. The artist made explicit the phallic connotation of this Madoura-designed water-jar by painting the vessel as a male nude, a rapidly achieved bit of playfulness which lacks the serious fervour of this supplicating and fresh image from Iran, of which little is known.

An imposing group of figures stand imperiously on a hollow base *(below)* – an upside-down pot. This is a tableau of a particular kind for it is an altar or shrine to the yam spirit, Ifijioku. He is an important deity, for yam is the most important crop among the Igbo people of Nigeria. It shows a chieftain and his family and in his hands he holds a horn and a fan, symbols that display his status, while on either side are his two pregnant wives, heavily scarified on face and breast, and with elaborate head pieces; they also hold fans. All three figures have necklaces and we can see the beauty of a second one on the woman to the right – serpent-like, ending in a bunch of small flowers. In front of them sits a child on a stool playing on a double gong, and a fowl, presumably the sacrifice. The pot in the middle is a shrine within a shrine and represents a receptacle to receive the offering. Behind the group is a screen with several decorative loops at its side.

There is a strong sense of linear rhythm and balanced texture in this work, a texture that has been built up simply by coils, which have been regularly tool-pressed, and impressed marks stamped on the faces and the fowl; there is also a little *sgraffito* on the horn. All these marks exhibit a rightness of scale and create a richness of surface with even the extra numerary fingers adding to the fullness of the decoration. Another such work, collected in 1880, was a common round-bottomed cooking pot around which similar figures drop down the outside from the rim, transforming it into a ritualistic cult object. Only a handful of such ceramics are known, made in the 19th and early 20th centuries,

English, Ian Godfrey, *Fox
Box*, 33 cm (13 in.),
1970–76

PHOTOGRAPH © BUCKINGHAM-
SHIRE COUNTY MUSEUM

and they are believed to have been made by women who were the ceramic workers in most of tropical Africa.

The contemporary potter, Ian Godfrey, has applied small modelled elements
to a deep-lidded drum-like 'box' *(above)*, populating his ceramic landscape with
dish-like flower forms, fox heads, ducks and houses. In this busy scene there is
not a human figure in sight. The foxes look out from the interior of the pot in
rows, the ducks feed outside the slabbed houses in the surroundings of huge full

blooming flowers, pinholed dots, studs and impressed circles on the grey, dry-glazed steepness of the hill. In his work he uses a wide range of references to other cultures and symbols from distant civilisations. In this piece, made in 1970, the store-houses with their overhanging eaves and the angular cut-out feet surely owe something to Chinese ceramics.

The idea of context, domestic tableaux and landscape is not an uncommon one, as we have seen it in the Igbo yam altar, and ceramic models have also been found elsewhere, mostly in tombs to comfort the dead.

In Egypt, during the Middle Kingdom (2040–1650BC), potters built miniature houses especially for the interred, together with servants and generous supplies of food. It was believed that these objects could, magically, be given life and so allow the dead to have perpetual ease without having to rely on the offerings of the living.

The notion of context is different in Etruria. In one example from 8th century BC, homely comfort derives from an urn made in the shape of a wattle and daub hut, explicitly designed with dormer windows, timbers protruding rhythmically from the roof and a door through which the ashes were deposited. Finally, the porticoed entrance was closed, allowing the dead to rest at home.

The lid of a green glazed stoneware 'hill jar' from 3rd century China is made in the shape of a mountain with a temple at its peak. Modelled elaborately with buildings and people in tiers, it probably illustrated their intended paradise in the western mountains.

In the Shang period, in China, not only precious objects but also servants, slaves and animals were buried with their masters to serve them in the next world. Gradually this grisly practice was replaced by the use of models. The most amazing and extravagant example of thus contextualising the world of the dead was the massive terracotta, underground army of Emperor Qin Shi Huang in Shanxi Province. Discovered by chance behind an apricot orchard, it was started in 246BC and took 36 years to build. Details of this discovery can be found in Chapter 5.

In the Han Dynasty (206BC–AD220) beautiful ceramic models of people, animals and domestic objects were made. An increasing interest in perpetuating both the objects and scenes of everyday life led to large-scale ceramic buildings being produced, often in a farming context. Elaborate models of these buildings and modelled figures were placed in tombs, in the expectation that they would extend the after-life to include the farming landscape. In the banqueting hall of a manor house, in one such model, sit a group of six small musicians as well as several dishes, plates and a jug as though ready for a feast. The owner of this grand building must have been a major landowner.

The example illustrated here (*opposite*) is from the Han Dynasty. As it is almost a metre (3 ft) high it has been made in three sections; and it shows clearly the excellence of early ceramic skill. It also clearly details many architectural features which were to be used in Chinese buildings for many centuries,

China, Han Dynasty,
model of storehouse,
95.2 cm (37½ in.),
206BC – AD220
PHOTOGRAPH © GLASGOW
MUSEUMS, THE BURRELL
COLLECTION

such as the complex bracketing system under the eaves, the patterned screens and other features. It includes two storemen climbing the stairs, having passed a relief sculpture on the way, while on the roof are two cockerels, perhaps living creatures or perhaps roof tiles. The house is lead-glazed and it seems that glazes were confined to mortuary pottery at this time. They are limpidly soft and do not obscure the detail; they are easily eroded and take on a silvery iridescence, which combined with the green of the copper, is a very pleasing, gentle addition.

The cockerels on the Han storehouse may indeed have been roof tiles, for ante-fixes and roof ornaments are found in many countries, including China, and are examples of some lively and notable ceramic art. They are used to mask the junction of a row of tiles or as gutter terminals, and are both practical and decorative and quite frequently had a cult function. In the past the roofs in China were made of brightly coloured ceramic tiles. The end ridge tiles had, and still have on some existing buildings, various figures standing on them to ward off evil spirits.

This fierce-faced demon (*right*) is a guardian of the house. Painted with enamel colours and glazed, it balances on the slope of the turquoise ridge tile, fist at the ready. Because its legs have to bear some weight it is steadied by the stool, or shell form, for support. Like so many roof ornaments it would have been formed from a mould thus allowing repeat motifs. This tile was made in the 16th or 17th century AD.

The lion's head (*below*), also a protective figure, is far earlier in date, coming

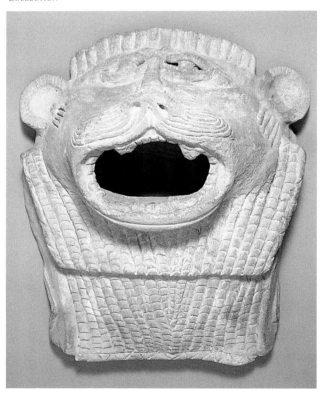

from the 2nd millennium BC. As it is designed with a flattened back, it was probably intended to be incorporated in a temple as a protective figure, for in archaic times the lion and the sphinx acquired special importance as the guardians of sanctuaries and funerary monuments.

It is a snarling creature with looping whiskers and flattened coils of clay are issuing from its nostrils and side mane, while the full mane and ears are incised, the eyes are modelled in detail and the open mouth with teeth, fangs and throat are alarmingly visible. This frightening beast, almost life-size, comes from the city state of Isin Larsa in Babylon.

It is not surprising that the lion, a terrifying, bellowing creature, was sometimes used to represent the goddess of thunder-storms as well as the power and majesty of the king. The lion's function as guardian, and its symbolic representations continued well into the Middle Ages.

The Etruscans placed heavy emphasis on the terracotta decorations of the roof and, although

China, demon roof tile,
41 cm (16 ⅛ in.), 16th–
17th century AD
PHOTOGRAPH © GLASGOW
MUSEUMS, THE BURRELL
COLLECTION

Etruscan, Cerveteri, head antefix, 26.8 cm, (10 ¼ in.), 520–500BC

they used building techniques inspired by the Greeks and were influenced by the Italian tradition of wooden embellishments to roofs, they found their own independent style of expression. They reached the highest level of achievement during the 6th century BC, with their creations including antefixes in the form of heads. They sometimes had a flat back, as in this 6th-century BC example from Cerveteri, while others were fully modelled. This moulded terracotta head is of a woman wearing a diadem and ear-rings. The wavy hair framing the face and the style of painting on the modelling is reminiscent of the head on the 5th-century Greek wine jug in this chapter (*see p.49*). Such sculptures might have been set all along the eaves of temples, masking the junction of the row of tiles, and painted in bright colours they would have been strikingly beautiful on the skyline. In spite of the freshness of the face this image can only hint at the brilliance of the colour at the time.

Roof ornaments are also found further afield. A 19th-century embellishment from the Sepic river valley in Papua New Guinea combines fired clay, straw and hair in a fertility figure which is seated on top of an inverted pot, alongside a mythological bird whose neck and bill top the image. It is a strange, primitive ritual object.

From Northern Nigeria comes this lively energetic female (*opposite, above*). She sits on a large upside down pot-form, spiked with pointed studs, with the lower part of the pot encircled by handles like those we have found on Nigerian cult objects and cooking-pots. The hole suggests that this roof finial may have been placed over the exit of a smoking fire. The figure with legs stretched out behind, and arms swinging in front, seems to have sprung onto the base at just this moment, giving a vital sense of movement to the figure.

The strange head has a hint of the high Nigerian hair-style, holes have been pierced for the eyes and in the disc-like ears, and the jawless mouth is thrust forward. A necklace of spiky studs surround the neck and larger but similarly modelled spikes form the breasts. The incised marks on the body are probably representative of the scarification marks of the tribe. Such an object may be kept in the burial hut over the tomb of the chief or on top of the hut's roof, and when the chief dies it is removed and wrapped in a white cloth until a new chief is appointed.

Gargoyles were common in medieval England and this cheeky face below with its tongue stuck out belongs to that genre. Dated from the 14th century AD it was found mounted on the ridge of a roof in Oxford's High Street. It is a chimney-pot, and the large gouged openings of eyes and ears, the slit mouth and nostrils all allowed the smoke to escape from the open hearth below. These heads are relatively rare and would only be found on the grander houses as each is uniquely modelled; we can tell that this has been fabricated by hand by the way the clay has been smoothed and the rough spontaneity which gives it such life. It would have been made of the same clay as the pantiles it topped and fired in the tiler's kiln. In Victorian times, of course, mass-produced moulded finials of dragons, heads and mythical creatures were very common.

Nigeria, pottery finial, 38 cm (15 in.), 1950s
PHOTOGRAPH © COPYRIGHT THE BRITISH MUSEUM

England, Medieval chimney pot, 14th century AD
PHOTOGRAPH © ASHMOLEAN MUSEUM, UNIVERSITY OF OXFORD

The Wassau cult object (*above*), from the East Sepic province of Papua New Guinea, bears a superficial resemblance to the medieval chimney-pot, though the intention and purpose for its creation are very different. The likeness lies in the cut-out orifices, the framed face with the whole topped by the pointed 'bobble'. Here the face and the pot are one, the features are cut out of the body and an added flange surrounds and isolates them; the long curved nose with side nostrils has also been added, and out of the opening at the top of the pot projects the hook-like plug which turns this small-based vessel into a closed, sculptural form.

The variety of pot-figures illustrated have been hand-built or moulded, with modelled additions. In 'Wine pitcher in the form of a cavalier', thrown elements have been combined to form this single vessel. Picasso designed and directed craftsmen to produce standard ceramic shapes – necks, handles, feet and bellies of traditional vases and pots – and to reassemble these components in order to create the birds, bulls, goats and figures that he had already conceived in drawings.

Here the three-dimensional composition is made up of a large, oval body placed at an angle on the base, with a long neck terminating in a bowl-form and two handles. It is boldly painted, with one colour, in such a way that the neck becomes the torso, the bowl the face and the strap handles the arms of the cavalier, while the full-bellied pot becomes the horse.

As in most of the other ceramic pieces in this chapter the balance between the vessel and the figurative element is poised and the general form of the vessel remains undisguised, reflecting its original function, while taking on the character of human or animal.

Pablo Picasso, wine pitcher, 42 cm (16 ½ in.), c.1950–51

4
Some Clay Figures in the Western Tradition

In the previous chapter, where the figure was fabricated from a pot, it was the outer edge of the space within the vessel that created the shape and the void that created the form. In traditional sculpture the image describes not only the solidity of the object but also an awareness of the underlying structure, maybe bone sinew, muscle or the skeleton.

The vessel's main attribute is volume while that of sculpture is mass. The mass exists in its own space, it looks inward, it does not connect through any kind of opening or orifice to the world outside itself. The vessel offers us participation – we can put things in it, drink from it, use it; even asymmetrical sculptural vessels are receptacles. The closed sculpture is self-contained, it distances us while inviting us to regard and inspect it. In the early 20th century, when concavities and holes were often incorporated into sculpture, they became other sculptural elements rather than voids. The Italian Futurist, Umberto Boccioni (1882–1916) declared: 'There must be a complete abolition of definite line and closed sculpture. We break open the figure and enclose within it the environment'.

Reasons for making sculpture over the ages have varied. They may be fertility objects, or overt gestures satisfying the need to make sense of the world; or they aim to synthesise random elements by making a visual unity of them, to see beyond the world and bear witness to gods as superior beings, giving them gifts or making their likeness, to connect the two worlds of life and death. They may adorn temples and sanctuaries, commemorate the lives of great men and heroes, idealise the image of man, make portraits, describe daily life, adorn buildings and the home, or comment on daily life.

Different civilisations had different attitudes to the making of images. The Sumerians believed that man was created for the benefit of the gods, so their images were conceived in human form and as though they had the same human desires and passions; thus any calamity on earth was taken to be a sign of divine

opposite:
Italy, Bernini, model for
Saint Longinus, *c.*1629–38
PHOTOGRAPH COURTESY OF: THE
FOGG ART MUSEUM, HARVARD
UNIVERSITY OF MUSEUMS,
ALPHEUS HYALL PURCHASING
AND FRIENDS OF THE FOGG
MUSEUM FUND

anger. As they were imagined to be in man's own image, Sumerians felt that their deities could be appealed to directly. Thus most of their works of art were designed to propitiate and serve.

The gods and goddesses in Indian sculpture, however, were representations of the sublime, and included innumerable semi-divine beings and demons. The images drew upon human, animal and bird forms and species were frequently combined to create composite creatures; there are countless statues communicating different aspects of the divine. In Buddhist and Hindu sculpture sacred representations were required to be beautiful, as it was believed that the deity might then be persuaded to inhabit their visible outer forms.

To please the gods, the Greeks also wanted to make beautiful sculpture, as they had an overwhelming belief that beauty was the greatest gift they could offer to the divine, and that the human body was the most beautiful thing known, believing it to be a common bond between god and man. As the gods did not grow old the sculpture is largely of youthful figures: in their sculpture man and god are interchangeable.

The representation of the human body and its beauty held no place in ethnic sculpture, neither was it to be seen in isolation or in a fixed place as in the monuments of Greece and Rome, except as architectural features such as house-posts or doors. Sculptural objects, which had a social and a ritualistic function, would be brought out only for ceremonies. For example, the masks of the Kalabari of the Nigeria Delta were used in performances associated with placating unpredictable water-spirits before a fishing expedition; apart from such occasions the masks were put away and were of no importance. Certain sculptures belonged to closely guarded secret societies and were quite unknown to some members of the small community. In the guild of carvers in the Benin court the actual act of making was sacred and the work was carried out in a ritual context.

Both Greek and ethnic sculpture had an outstanding influence on Western art, from Classical and Archaic Greek art through the early Romans and the Italians of the 15th and 16th centuries, and the sculpture of Africa and, to a lesser degree the Pacific, through artists working in the first decade of the 20th century, in particular Pablo Picasso and his associates.

To return to Greece, we find that the great medium of the early Archaic phase was painted terracotta, which continued to be dominant in Corinth and in the Greek colonies in Italy. However, the independent Etruscans were also totally influenced by the monumental style of Greek art, including the hollow casting in bronze. They controlled metal-rich Toscana and, like their exemplars, became renowned for their bronze work. Unfortunately little of this remains as much was melted down in antiquity and in medieval times, so that their sculpture is now represented by terracotta figures or carvings in their native stone. Their clay figures were largely used to decorate temples along with ornamental antefixes (*see p.62*). The life-sized sculptures stood on the roof beams of the heavily proportioned and deep-porched Tuscan temples, and were created partly for rituals which called for observations of the skies, and partly to illustrate mythological scenes.

Opposite:
Etruscan Veii, Goddess and child, 1.43m (5 ft 1 in.), 500BC
PHOTOGRAPH © SOPRINTENDENZA ARCHEOLOGICA PER L'ETRURIA MERIDIONALE, ROME

This goddess and child (*right*) come from the outstanding group of figures that once decorated the Potonaccio temple of Veii, north of Rome and built by the Etruscans in 500BC. Here, staggered along the length of the roof beam several statues act out a tug-of-war between Apollo and Hercules who tries to carry off the hind of Apollo's sister, Artemis. This image of mother and child, thought to be part of that scene, is fleeing from the fight. Her face bears the soft, human smile which is found typically in archaic Greek sculpture of the same period. It was the emotionalism of Hellenistic art rather than the more intellectual aspects of calculated proportion or the scientific study of movement that appealed to the Etruscans. In fact the proportions of this figure are strange in that the long legs and torso are surmounted by a small head. Is it likely that the unusual perspective created by the siting of the statue well above eye-level was deliberately exaggerated? The goddess is held upright by sturdy, thrusting, faceted legs and by a support that anchors the weight on the base and allows the flat-backed figure to stand tall. The left arm is broken, probably at the juncture of a join, and we can see how the shoulder and arm grow out of the back-rest. The beautiful head is fully modelled, with the downcast eyes heavily accented by the eyebrows and continuous with the bridgeless chiselled nose, and a bony hand holds the child's legs. Like the antefix of the previous chapter, the woman wears a diadem on her head above the careful waves of the hair. This regularly patterned hairstyle neatly framing the clear forehead and then drawn back behind the ears is found in many of the carved sculptures in archaic Greece, usually on young men (kouroi) and sometimes on women (korai). In stone or marble the limitations of the carving tool, probably a punch, have led to a series of stylised bobbles for the hair. If this is such an adaptation of style the immediacy of these scalloped locks has retained all the freshness of thumbed clay; the swirling hem of the dress repeats the idea of scallops while the shell-like folds of the garment cling to the wide hips. The exquisite

precision of the modelling, emphasising light and shade, and the gilding give life and drama to this temple decoration.

Archaic art described types not individuals, but the enigmatic, mysterious smile, common in this period, lights up the secret, serene inner happiness and vitality of this sculpture. The whole group of sculptures has been attributed to Vulca of Veii, the only Etruscan known by name.

The Etruscans also made splendid terracotta and stone sarcophagi and cinerary urns. The base, a box or coffin holding the ashes or body of the dead, was often carved or had modelled panels in relief around it and an inscription upon the lid or chest which might include the subject's name, age and history. In this example the writing around the bottom of the cask identifies the figure as *Seianti Hanunia Tlesnasa*. Often there are conjugal couples modelled on the lid, but she is on her own. These figures either lie recumbent as though in sleep or, more generally, recline on pillows as if at a banquet. Sometimes the heads are modelled in the idealised manner of Hellenistic portraits and some are more realistic, with many, like Seianti painted in bright colours. Clearly this was a well-to-do lady, her jewellery – a tiara, ear-rings, necklace, bracelets and rings – are painted yellow, suggesting that they were made of gold. More extravagantly, her family commissioned a sculptor to fashion her likeness, and it is known that

Etruscan, sarcophagus (Seianti), 1.83 m (4 ft), 150–130BC
PHOTOGRAPH © COPYRIGHT THE BRITISH MUSEUM

another sarcophagus was found belonging to another woman in her family. With her right hand, and showing her heavy bejewelled arm, Seianti draws back her veil like a young bride, while in the other she holds a mirror which she does not look into as she stares at us – a vain young lady.

When the coffin was opened it was found to contain the body of an old lady together with a silver mirror, a scraper, a lidded box, a flask and an oval vessel hung from nails fixed to the wall of the tomb. Of its manufacture little is known. At 1.83 m (6 ft.) it is large, the size of a coffin. It appears to have been fired in several parts, the figure and the couch in two pieces, the lid in two pieces and the base apparently in one. One can only assume that there must have been a fixed wood-fired kiln that was capable of accommodating this and the large votive statues.

Even after the Etruscans were assimilated into the Roman world and the common language of Latin was spoken, artistic and social traditions were retained in Etrurian cities, and the production of stone and terracotta sarcophagi and cinerary urns continued to be made by many local artists. The practice lasted from the 6th to the 1st century BC. This is a late work dated somewhere between 150 and 130BC.

In Classical Greece a legacy from the Archaic period meant that large clay sculptures continued to be made, but these were not common. It was the time of great monumental sculptural works in marble, bronze and stone and of architectural masterpieces using Ionic, Corinthian and Doric orders. It was these that were to have such a profound influence on the development of Western art.

With the mastery of techniques in casting and carving, clay sculpture was now found mainly in small figures, clay reliefs and plaques, but whatever the scale, material or purpose there was a unity of style informing the work of each generation. Because of the surprising mobility among sculptors innovations were quickly assimilated and this common approach can be recognised in the small clay figures which closely matched and frequently copied works in marble. There were also original studies of humans and animals, and subjects ignored by sculptors in marble of a more everyday nature – figures of actors, hollow masks, or studies of dancers. These small clay objects have added to our knowledge of Greek life and sculpture which would otherwise have been lost. They have been found in sanctuaries as votive offerings to the gods and goddesses who gained in importance until they became the focal point of Hellenic life; as well as serving as a dedication in graves or sanctuaries they were also becoming more common in the home. The western Greeks were expert at making fine moulds for such figures, and combined with the high quality of the original modelling this led to some surprising small masterpieces in fired clay.

The early Classical figure of the late 5th century BC (*overleaf*), probably from Boeotia, is of a fleeing woman. She stands on a 7 cm (2 ¾ in.) rectangular base which in no way restricts the rapid movement created by her bent left knee, the thrust of the right leg and the billowing folds of her veil blown behind her back by her rapid motion. Drapery, a strong feature in classical sculpture which could

Greek, Boeotia, fleeing
woman, 31 cm (12 ¼ in.),
5th century BC

be rendered most skilfully in marble, is used here to emphasise twisting poses, with folds running counter to each other, and with a transparency that shows the well-formed modelling of the body underneath. The material of her baggy-sleeved linen chiton hangs vertically in string-like folds between the legs and, like the veil, flies behind her back. While the lower half of the body below the flat belt is so clearly moving to the right the upper part does not but is still front-facing – it is the haloeing veil that frames the figure and suggests action. This pose, with one leg relaxed and the weight of the body shifted onto the other is known as *contrapposto* and marks off the Classical from the Archaic pose, becoming a strong theme in 15th century sculpture. This figure of pale red clay, with visible remains of white slip, is not totally three-dimensional but is hollowed out at the back.

As man was the measure of all things to the Greeks early Greek sculptors were less interested in the female figure than in the male. Nudity was their natural expression of admiration for the perfectly developed male body, which represented both their warriors and their heroic gods. The realism of the naked form would have been heightened by the colour painted on them. In contrast, the idealism with which the female form was created eliminated detail – although the transparent drapery which leaves the body almost naked continued to be popular.

As the study of anatomy gave way to a clearer knowledge of skeletal and muscular systems in the 5th century BC, an important basic principle emerged which revolutionised sculpture. It was that body motion is interrelated, that one part cannot move without affecting the others. Now that the movement of the body could be explained mechanistically, new poses in the Hellenistic studies of femininity found goddesses crouching, figures leaning in spiral compositions, and bodies which could be arrested in motion. With these new possibilities one-view figures were discarded by the 4th century BC; they were now seen fully in the round with the twist of the body inviting viewers to walk around the sculpture, as no one position provided a complete view.

In the clay model (*overleaf*) of the bathing Aphrodite of 200BC from Taranto in southern Italy the figure bends slightly forward and twists to the left, the left leg carrying the weight while the right is bent at the knee and is raised. This is a pose similar to those of other Aphrodite figures binding or unbinding their sandals, and is of a type found among terracotta figures and bronzes of the period. The shoulders are at a steep angle and we can see how, throughout the length of the body, there is compensatory muscular adjustment through the breasts, the navel and the crotch which are all at slightly different angles. By the time the knees are reached we are able to see that they are at a contrary angle from the shoulders. In bending to the left the body is scrunched while the right side is extended at full stretch.

The upper part of the body is slender, with well modelled breasts, and the heavier hips and natural, fleshy stomach are subtly modelled, leading to the sturdy legs and thighs. Even without arms, head or left ankle and foot this is a

Greek, Taranto, bathing
Aphrodite, 18 cm (7 ⅛ in.),
200BC

striking image of arrested motion and in spite of its small size it has a monumentality which defies scale.

Like the figure of Aphrodite this horse's head was moulded by a coroplast from Taranto in the late 5th or early 4th century BC. A great many moulds of similar heads have been found; they have a certain affinity with the spirited horses on the Parthenon frieze and in this particular period it was common for small scale terracotta sculptures to reflect major monuments. This is a fine and lively example: the delicately modelled and well understood features of the head are hollow and mould-made, but the mane may have been added by hand, for the thick, shaggy tool-marked locks have a more urgent and rougher appearance than the rest.

Inspired by the new Hellenistic art an important group of miniature figures in clay which closely copied well known types of major sculpture were produced in Asia Minor, with the best known examples coming from Smyrna in Syria.

This head (*overleaf*), made in the 1st century BC and only 12 cm (4 ¾ in.) high is very similar in type to a larger than life-size portrait statue of a prince, thought to be Demetrius I of Syria, made in the 2nd century BC. The Greek idealisation which illustrates

Greek, Taranto, horse's head, ht. 9 cm (3 ½ in.), d. 11 cm (4 ⅜ in.), 5th or early 4th century BC
PHOTOGRAPH © ASHMOLEAN MUSEUM, UNIVERSITY OF OXFORD

Syria, Smyrna, male head, 12 cm (4 ¾ in.), 1st century BC

such abstract concepts as statesmanship or intellectual power has been combined with realism in this perplexed, frowning, somewhat arrogant head. As in the original figure the portrait head was once part of a full statue, as the well preserved clay surface shows remains of gilding, presumably aping the material of the original. This was a figure in the round, with the back carefully modelled and continuing the curly locks which frame the wide furrowed brow. The head is modelled in such a way that the light and shade have been deliberately enhanced by the set-back eyes, the outward thrust of the full lower lip and the deep cleft under it.

The Greeks painted some parts of their marble sculptures, above all the dress, hair and eyes. It was not until the Hellenistic period that a way was found to represent the eye by purely sculptural means. We can see here how the deep-set eyes allow the brow to shadow them, and the cutting of a hole for the eyeball above the puffy lid gives 'colour' to the head and a realism in the commanding intensity of this man's stare.

The influence of Greek art was widespread, but not only on Western art. It was carried by Alexander the Great (356–323BC) into Egypt, Mesopotamia, Central Asia and India and eventually to Pakistan. An important school of Greco-Buddhist sculpture arose in Gandhara – modern Pakistan – which influenced the arts of India and to some degree those of Buddhist China.

The indelible mark left on Western sculpture by Greek art inspired a second flowering 2000 years later. There was a renewed interest in the art and culture of Greece, Rome and Etruria in the 15th century, with artists such as Donatello and Piero della Francesca taking up the Greek ideas of vitality, beauty, bodily proportion, movement and gesture, and fusing them with realism to produce a new representation. It was a rebirth or renaissance of the art of antiquity.

It was the discovery of classical texts in Western Europe which led to the foundation of Italian Renaissance humanism. This was not strictly an art-historical phenomenon, as many of the finest figures were scholars and writers. Nevertheless, artists were able to take up the tradition of classical art with a surprising spirit of understanding which spanned the centuries and seemed a logical succession to it.

There are relatively few surviving Hellenistic or Greek originals, as apart from the many which were plundered, most of the bronzes were melted down in late antiquity and early medieval times, while the marble statues and reliefs were steadily burned in lime kilns. The main intermediary for our knowledge of them was the technically brilliant art of the Roman Empire, which first extensively plundered and then fostered Greek art. They knew it through the Greek colonies of Italy and Sicily, but it was the Etruscans who made the biggest contribution to the broad stream of European culture by their early adoption of it; the Roman appreciation of Greek art preserved it for Western civilisation. Fortunately there was an early demand in Rome for the most famous masterpieces. Most of the pastiches made by the Greeks – and there was a thriving industry of copiers – did not survive. The Romans meanwhile often made free translations, adapting the work to suit the new taste. For example, Venus, a popular subject, might be produced with the portrait head of a Roman matron. Furthermore the sculpture was largely made in marble even when the originals were in bronze, gold, ivory or wood, and needed struts and supports – such as tree trunks – unnecessary in the bronze originals. In spite of adaptation in pose, expression and material they were probably most accurate. There was one way, however, in which the Roman model drastically altered the perception of Greek sculpture. The Greeks invariably painted their work while the Romans introduced white uncoloured marble. This is what we see today, not only in classical sculpture, but in all the monuments of the Renaissance and later.

The notion that the carving of stone, particularly of marble, was the highest aim and greatest achievement of sculptors was assimilated throughout Europe and beyond. It began with the Egyptian and Babylonian civilisations, was reinforced by the Greeks, the Romans and the Italians and remains in the common consciousness today. Nevertheless, clay had a place even in major works, where modelling in soft materials had an important intermediary role. Before embarking on a major work the artist could take advantage of the plastic character of clay or wax, and these could be manipulated with speed to grasp or generate fleeting ideas.

We know that one of the greatest Renaissance figures, Michelangelo (1475–1564), used this method and also used pen and ink sketches or black and red chalk drawings to clarify his thoughts. The models were also used for reference while he was working on marble and gave patrons some idea of how the finished project would look. The number of his original models in clay, though not large, is remarkable, particularly as they are very fragile as they have not been fired but are described as 'sun baked'.

He was by no means the first to use models; indeed it has been assumed that the Greeks used clay models to clarify the general planning and to instruct artists who carried out the extensive sculptural programmes on the temples, which included the Parthenon. Michelangelo's models were quite different from those that went before as they are less finished, wonderfully immediate and rapidly worked three-dimensional sketches, made for himself alone. They have a tremendous appeal to contemporary sensibilities.

Although *The Youthful Captive* illustrated (*opposite*) is in red wax, it looks very similar in surface technique and expresses the essential pose in the same way as a *bozzetto* – or model – in clay. In spite of the evident speed of execution the *contrapposto* figure with head on one side circled by the bent arm, the muscular legs and the twisted body give a clear and vivid description for the intended carving, and indeed the final marble corresponds very closely to it. Michelangelo was always aware of the final object which existed within the marble block, like the antique sculptures in which he immersed himself during the time he spent in Rome. For him, releasing the figure from the marble, using its extreme edges, was the ideal way of producing pure sculpture.

Another great artist of the Late Renaissance, Bernini (1598–1680) effortlessly dominated the artistic scene, monopolising papal commissions during Rome's 'Golden Age'. Some of his models have survived, and it is evident that he handled clay with remarkable dexterity and rapidity, producing many clay sketches at tremendous speed for each of his highly prestigious commissions: one clay model after another helped to clarify the first general idea. These *bozzetti* assumed a central position in his creative process. While the immediate expression of an idea was resolved through the medium of clay, the execution was carried out in marble; much of the physically hard work of transferring the sketch to marble was carried out by assistant sculptors in his workshops. Like artists since the second half of the 16th century Bernini's imagination was focused on the swirling curves of the Baroque which he achieved with virtuosity and delicacy. However, unlike the Mannerists of a generation before, he did not use the new ideal of sculpture to make work with many views of equal importance, but rather to fix a moment of exuberant energetic action. It was necessary for the spectator to stand in the correct position to get the full impact of the climax of the drama.

For the statue of Saint Longinus (*on p.66*), a contemporary of Bernini records that he saw at least 22 small models in the studio, and of these only this one has survived. The final larger than life-sized marble statue is in St. Peter's Basilica in Rome, where it can be seen that the composition of the model is completed by an outflung hand on the left arm, with a tall spear held by the right hand starting near the right foot and finishing well above the head. In spite of the originality of the pose with the spread-eagled arms, the stance of the figure and the folds of the garment are in typical classical tradition, and it was to the classical form that Bernini reverted when he was struggling with a new commission. But although the marble version is akin to this model, the balance was altered by having the legs more equally weighted, and the relative calm of the folds was replaced by more expressively flamboyant and rhythmic drapery which cascaded

down to the ground. Bernini had transposed the classical origins of the work to a more emotionally charged and personal style.

Flying drapes, outflung hands and swooning figures were forms that exceeded the boundaries of a block of marble, so it was necessary to add or extend with more than one block to capture the richness of movement inspired by the active manipulation of clay. Bernini considered that his greatest achievement was making the hard marble as flexible as wax, clay or flesh.

Modelling had freed the imagination, allowing it to portray the restless emotion of the Baroque; in the middle of the 16th century the modeller had became the creator, and the artist who worked the stone was now a skilled craftsman or technician.

It is not surprising that relatively few of the 1000 models produced by Bernini have survived, for they were really only rough working notes and fragile, and would have been fired in the kilns of potters making low-fired pieces such as pots or tiles. Those that exist are little known but some can be found in the Hermitage Museum in St. Petersburg and, like Saint Longinus, in the Fogg Museum of Harvard University.

In 1666 the French Academy of Rome was founded and the ageing Bernini was asked to keep a benevolent eye on it. French students flocked to Rome, and while some returned to France, others remained and in spite of the continuing importance of Bernini and the Roman Baroque, French influence increased rapidly: sculpture was becoming more international.

The French sculptor Louis François Roubiliac (1702–62) settled in England in 1730, bringing with him the characteristics of the finest European rococo style, which had grown out of the Baroque. He visited Rome in 1752 and, for the first time saw Bernini's work: it had a profound effect on him. Roubiliac had already made a name for himself in England with his first commission – a statue of George Frideric Handel (1685–1759). Funerary monuments were produced on a grand scale in France and England during the middle of the 18th century; in England Westminster Abbey was the most prestigious location for such commemorative work, and today Handel's marble monument can be seen here, along with other work by Roubiliac. The statue of the composer, initially erected in Vauxhall Pleasure gardens in 1738, was eventually installed in the Abbey in 1762.

The image here shows what was probably the final clay model for the full-scale marble monument. It is highly finished in detail and surface, with the alert realistic head, the carefully modelled hands and the textures of the fabrics all directed to the final appearance in marble. The head of Handel, a man in his 50s, is probably a portrait, for the sculptor had a reputation for his lively and naturalistic portraiture. There is a twist to the rather solid body and one foot reaches out beyond the step towards the viewer – a device used with far more aggression in later and more monumental works. Appropriate objects allow Handel to lean diagonally; he holds a manuscript in his left hand and with the right he points to a figure above: David with a harp. The whole tableau combines relief, bas-relief

French, Roubiliac, model
for the Handel monument,
98 cm (38 ¾ in.), 18th
century

and three-dimensional form which exists in shallow space; there is one best viewpoint.

In this final model, of course, clay is used as a means to an end and at this stage the actual tactile and other material chacteristics of clay are not exploited. The smooth, clear definition of the surface is close to that of the final marble. It is a realistic and complete homage to Handel.

Later sculptors such as Bourdelle, Degas and Matisse, led by Rodin, ignored the academic use of the sketch as preliminary to another final work. The immediate clay modelling with its rough finish, alive with visible additions, rough gouges and finger marks, was the final work; process and essential expression were integrated. The best way of preserving the detail of these inventions and their passionate spontaneity was by casting them in bronze, where the special calligraphy of each artist's working of the soft material shows clearly.

Auguste Rodin (1840–1917) was the forerunner in casting from the directly formed model, making no attempt to hide or smooth the loosely modelled surfaces. The Greeks, Michelangelo and the human figure were central to his creed as a sculptor but, like Bernini, Rodin was one of the greatest modellers in the history of sculpture and, although skilled himself, he rarely worked the stone. When he became successful and demand for his work grew, most of the marble carving was left to his many assistants, who numbered among them such eminent younger sculptors as Charles Despiau and Emile-Antoine Bourdelle. They would have carved the several versions of *The Kiss*, for example, and possibly the original executed in 1886.

Rodin always worked from the nude model and in his quest for movement he used many who walked around the studio, where he sketched them from different angles and positions. When a movement attracted him the pose was held and he took a piece of clay and made a *maquette*. Rodin modelled from all viewpoints, so his sculpture needs to be seen from all sides: not for him the static viewer. He claimed that he only copied what he saw; his inspiration was faithful to his sensations.

Most of the important sculptors of the first half of the 20th century could not avoid responding to the work of Rodin, often in reaction to its romantic excesses, but he did radically change the attitudes of succeeding sculptors. We have already seen how the correspondence between the material process of execution and imaginative expression was integrated in the final creation.

Another far-reaching innovation involved a move away from the whole figure: *La Centauresse* of 1884, for example *(right)*, is an armless torso. Although artists and students had copied fragments of antiquity since the 16th century, Rodin was the first to explore the concept that parts of the body could stand for the whole in a finished work, that a complete body need not pre-suppose the full figure, that a torso, say, on its own, could be as expressive as a face. The ideal figure could be broken down so that a part could become a thing in its own right, and not merely a component. His smaller studies, often of parts of the body, were placed on shelves or tables and could be picked up and turned in the hand, so that all viewpoints could be appreciated and no one orientation was supreme.

Since Greek and Roman times statues were placed on pedestals which were often elaborately designed by architects; nobody up to this time had questioned this means of isolating and ennobling the work of art by doubling its size. In his wish to bring the figure to life, Rodin exhibited a life-size bronze sculpture, *Eve*, in the Paris Salon of 1897 and buried its base in the earth floor of the hall so that it became one with the spectators. The removal of sculpture from its pedestal in some measure released it from its preciousness and separation from life. Startling at the time, his ideas pointed to a new way of seeing, and eventually became one of the means to a pure abstraction of form.

Well-known painters who modelled in wax and clay but whose works were largely cast in bronze included Renoir, Matisse, and occasionally Braque. When Degas died in 1917, 150 wax or clay models were found in his studio. Gauguin made small stoneware models and Picasso produced a whole oeuvre of fired ceramics as well as some which were cast in bronze.

French, Auguste Rodin, *La Centauresse*, 21.5 cm (8 ½ in.), 1884 (S.990)

5
Other Traditions

Many young artists at the beginning of the 20th century rejected much that had gone before – the classical ideal which had become overstrained, the 'impressionism' of Rodin, and the reliance on the model and nature. Looking beyond the restraints of the Western tradition they discovered that in the art of Africa, the far East, pre-Columbian art and the origins of art before classical antiquity, there was a freedom divorced from the rationality of Greek Classical sculpture – an alternative to illusionism. Artists such as Picasso, Derain, Matisse and Brancusi saw in the museums of ethnography that the realistic proportions of the classical figure could be redefined and judged through their feelings and aesthetic intuitions. And at the same time, they recognised the possibility of abstraction. They saw in these calm powerful presences that did nothing significant with their bodies, an antidote to man in motion that had occupied previous generations. They also considered how far the human form could be fundamentally simplified to achieve its identity – a theme explored, for example, by Brancusi and Modigliani.

In these alien figures, too, it was possible to experience the sense of the mysterious and awesome in life, the irrational force that had made sculpture potent which was touched upon in Chapter 1. Picasso was particularly affected by this aspect; in 1907 he paid a visit to an ethnographic museum in Paris and later recalled: 'Men had made these masks for a sacred purpose, a magic purpose, as a kind of mediation between themselves and the unknown hostile forces that surround them . . . [painting] is a way of seizing power by giving form to our terrors as well as our desires.'

This new interest was aroused when numerous objects reached Europe at the end of the 19th century. For the first time tribal sculpture came to be regarded not as curios or barbaric objects brought back by travellers, merchants or missionaries, but as art. Artists now viewed it aesthetically as an escape from the predominantly academic art which they now felt the need to reject. Its local significance, largely undocumented, would not have been a prime consideration. Those artists who were inspired by these original and expressive forms were not, of course, necessarily looking at fired clay artefacts. Picasso's masks would have been carved out of wood, which was the dominant medium of African art. Most of these would have been lost through destruction by termites, had not the pioneering ethnographers of the turn of the century collected so massively. The

very occasional fragments which survive serve to show us what has been irrevocably lost.

The history of sub-Saharan sculpture is based mainly on the discoveries and researches of the last 80 or 90 years. So at the beginning of the 20th century artists would not, for example, have seen the highly sophisticated terracotta heads and figures of Nok, the oldest culture of black Africa dating from somewhere between 500BC and AD200. It was not until 1944 that these were discovered. Neither would they have seen the bronze heads from Benin which were initially discovered in 1910. As in most archaeologial discoveries chance and accident played a large part and it was clay and stone that survived.

This head (*left*) was not discovered until 1929 during the building of a prison at Luzira on the shores of Lake Victoria in Uganda. It was found among a collection of 14 terracotta objects which it was thought had originally made up four figures. Nothing similar has been found in the whole area and as the plastic arts are uncommon in East Africa they are unique. Luzira was the site of a shrine and it is thought that the figures were shrine furniture and that the many pot sherds – there were 150 found with them – were either an offering or the belongings of the priest or priestess.

The head with its associated torso do not necessarily belong together although they do appear to match well; a third section would have completed the body. The emphasis is on the large head, which, typical of African proportions, is a third to a quarter of the whole. It is strangely triangular; the protruding upper and lower lids, the eyebrows and the mouth have been modelled on, and the nose may have been drawn out from the main clay mass. The highly textured hair may represent a wig, or hair dressed in clay – a common practice among priests

Africa, Uganda, Luzira figure, 38 cm (15 in.)

or the ritual leaders. The body appears to be slightly narrower than the neck which is ringed by a necklace of diminishing size. The two small nipples are all that identify the lower portion as the torso. The head, aloof on the pedestal body, is a mysterious and enigmatic object.

The two sections of the Luzira head measure 38 cm (15 in.) in height. In the whole of black Africa, so far as is known, it is only in Nigeria, in the Nok and Ife cultures, that figures approaching life-size have been attempted. In the ancient civilization of Nok, which existed before the Christian era, figures were made that may have been more than 13.2 m (4 ft.) tall. To make them so finely and to fire them successfully required great technological skill. A coarse clay was used, which could withstand the vagaries of the bonfire or, one could speculate, although there is no evidence for it, that there may have been some form of kiln. The potter is the wife of the blacksmith in many areas of sub-Saharan Africa and he would have needed a furnace for making iron. With few exceptions ceramic sculpture is the work of potters, almost invariably women, using the coiling method, a technique discovered in some Nok sculpture and one which is still used by women today. The Nok sculpture is quite distinctive, the sandy coloured clay is pocked with coarse stony *engobe*; some faces, bearded, have infantile features representing the agelessness of their immortal ancestors. Others, more sophisticated and highly stylised, are characterised in particular by triangular-shaped eyes, by the hair-styles – often five buns on the geometrically stylised head – a style still used by African women today; the eye pupils, nostrils, lips and ears are normally pierced through the clay. The oldest examples found in clay have been discovered in tin mines and in the surrounding area of Nok.

Perhaps some of the greatest examples of black African art are found in the bronzes and terracottas of Ife, where many art-producing tribes of different cultures lived. Some experts believe that there is a link between the Nok and Ife traditions in spite of a time gap. Although findings show that Ife existed from about AD800 or even earlier, the naturalistic classical art of Ife flourished from the 11th or 12th century into the 14th or 15th century, contemporary with the European Renaissance, and indeed it has been compared with it and the other great naturalistic traditions of ancient Greece and Rome. From dating techniques applied to excavated heads it seems that the art of Ife developed first in terracotta and was then translated into metal as a fully realised style.

The very fine heads cast in bronze or brass, using the lost wax technique, and those made in clay belonging to the high classical period are unique in Africa in their realism; portrait-like, they appear to depict the actual physical characteristics of individuals rather than offering a generalised image. Of the two, the terracotta sculptures are far more numerous and show more variety of style. Some are naturalistic, some stylised and others are abstract; they also vary in scale from something close to life-size down to about 25 cm (10 in.). Some were made as free-standing heads, others come from complete figures, and all the Ife sculptures in bronze and terracotta were probably originally painted.

The free-standing head (*overleaf*) reveals the delicate modelling typical of the highest quality of Ife sculpture. It bears the characteristic vertical lines engraved regularly down the face which are found both in clay and metal, either a scarification no longer found among the Yoruba or their neighbours or, it has been suggested, that these striations might represent the veil worn by the chief. Other common features are the gentle modelling of the eyebrows and eyes with the distinctive feature of the upper lid overhanging the lower, the raised edges around

the beautiful fullness of the lips and the grooves around the neck. The subtle plumpness of the high-boned cheeks are fluently formed and the ears are carefully observed and placed. The headgear on these sculptures is variable: some are caps with holes pierced into them to hold feathers; a head of a queen wears a five-tiered ceramic modelled beaded crown. This scalloped head-dress, cap or hair, may also denote status. The sensitive and elegant outline of the profile and the thoughtful detached expression is typical of the Ife representation of the human head.

Now in the British Museum, this head was found in 1938, and as the first scientific excavations were not carried out until 1949 it is therefore one of the few pieces of Ife sculpture outside of Nigeria, for the bulk of all such objects unearthed to date are now in the Ife Museum.

Of all ancient Nigerian traditions Benin presents us with the largest body of sculptural work, and perhaps the best known. However, the fine heads, the delicate plaques and magnificent animals with which we are familiar have been cast in bronze using the lost wax technique so do not rightfully have a place here; yet the connection between Ife and Benin and between the cast works of Benin and the terracottas is worthy of note. The very earliest bronzes, according to oral tradition, were cast in Ife until the Oba of Benin requested a master caster, Igu'egha, to come to his court and establish the industry there towards the end of the 14th century. The naturalism of the Ife figures may have been transmitted but there was already an established art tradition, so doubtless its conventions were carried over when the technique of casting was introduced, for the sculpture of Benin is very distinct in subject matter and style from that of Ife, and it is the earliest castings which are considered to be the most naturalistic and beautiful.

While the bronzes were court art, made for the palace of the Oba, the little known heads in clay appear to have been non-royal equivalents of the bronzes (*see right*). It seems likely that it was only the chiefs of the bronze workers who were given the privilege of using heads like the Oba for their own ancestor cult.

Africa, Nigeria, Ife head, 29 cm (11 ⅜ in.), 13th century
PHOTOGRAPH © COPYRIGHT THE BRITISH MUSEUM

Opposite:
Africa, Nigeria, Benin head, 21 cm (8 ¼ in.), 15th century
PHOTOGRAPH © COPYRIGHT THE BRITISH MUSEUM

This early piece, 21 cm (8 ¼ in.) closely follows the style and ornamentation, the hair-style and the scarification found on the royal model.

This head (*left*), too, is probably a memorial sculpture collected from a graveyard over 180 years ago. It is larger than life-size, being 37.5 cm (14 ¾ in.) high. It comes from Northern Ewe country in Ghana and was made by the Kwaha, an Ashanti group living there at the time. It is not realistic as is the Ife head, as the eyes and mouth do not appear to emerge from the head as in the modelling, but are added on with strips or pellets of clay rather in the manner of the Luzira head. However, the placing of the features and the proportions of the head carry their own realism. The flattened discs of the ears break the gentle silhouette which rises up from the straight ringed neck to the widening curve of the face and cap. The satisfying simplicity of the head-covering may be accounted for by the fact that Ghana was converted to Islam in the 11th century. Whatever its history there is a harmony in the still calm of this dignified and serenely beautiful piece.

The open-mouthed male figure from Northern Nigeria (*right*) is part of a grave-marker, broken from a large spherical pot on which it stood. It would have been placed on the family tomb, a mound in which a man, his wives and his unmarried daughters would have been buried. Ordinary men would have domestic pottery placed on their graves, only a distinguished one would have been allowed such a notable memorial – a figure, perhaps, of one of his servants. The heavily scarified body was, at one time, typical of the Dakakari people. The sorrowing man, with head flung back, sings or wails, mourning the death of his master and family, while marking his grave.

Africa, Ghana, Ashanti head, 38 cm (15 in.), *c.* 19th century
Photograph © copyright
The British Museum

Prehispanic art never had a single moment of discovery in Europe unlike the startling effect that African art had around 1905. It was not until well into the 20th century, as Modern art was generating new aesthetic ideas, that these works became a source of inspiration to some Europeans. Again, unlike the African phenomenon which re-routed aesthetic thinking, it was current European style that determined which aspects of prehispanic art should be explored. It was, for example, the more angular and stylised traditions of Mesoamerica that were of interest to modernist artists during the first half of the 20th century. A British sculptor who was captivated by the power and simplicity of the stone carvings of the Mexican Mayan artists, was Henry Moore (1899–1986). These had a direct influence on his early work which continued throughout his life.

The best known work from pre-Columbian time is the Aztec from Mesoamerica and the Inca from the Andes. One of the least known areas archaeologically, Western Mexico, comprises five states which occupy much of the Pacific coast. Its inhabitants are known to have been sedentary farmers from early times and they produced ceramic vessels and human and animal figures. No buildings of the early pre-classical survive but the architecture of their temples and houses is known through clay models. These, and the figures, supply cultural information; they show a variety of activities and various types of ornaments, clothing and implements. From 500BC to AD600 one tradition that was unique to Western Mexico was the use of tomb and shaft chambers. Here, in the shaft or well leading to the tomb and concealed by earth-covered slabs, funerary ceramics were found. Although there must have been a strong symbolic meaning, such as a cult honouring of the dead, the figures were overtly naturalistic and secular, a celebration in clay of aspects and anecdotes of everyday life. Subjects included pregnant women, young figures performing daily tasks, rituals and warriors, and in the same direct and matter-of-fact way, images of the deformed such as hunchbacks and sick people who were considered to bring good luck.

One of the most unusual specimens of Mexican clay sculpture is found in Jalisco and the adjacent region of Nayarit, where the figure overleaf comes from. This seated woman is supported by her feet and two stool legs which are incorporated quite naturally into her leaning body; many of these figures seem to be sitting at ease on the ground, crouching or squatting. She has the characteristic tall, elongated head, but not the long narrow nose, which is associated with the ideal beauty of this definite racial type. She is elaborately adorned with a plain nose-ring and with decorative earplugs which

Africa, Northern Nigeria, grave-marker, 41 cm (16 ⅛ in.), early 20th century
PHOTOGRAPH © COPYRIGHT THE BRITISH MUSEUM

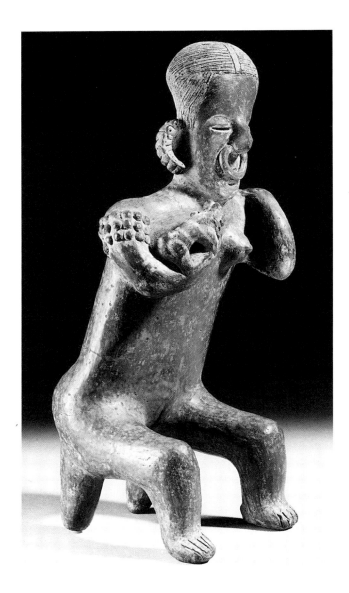

have been most lovingly modelled; scarification studs on her arms were also a popular form of body ornament. The hair with the neat parting has been scratched into the domed skull. The features are schematic, with slits for the eyes and mouth; the open mouth suggests that she is singing or chanting. The coil arms are short and unstructured and in the right one she clasps a small dog, while in her left hand she holds a plate which rests on her shoulder. The high breast is well modelled but there is no modelling on the unclothed, flattened body. These well-fired sculptures are made from a fine, high-quality, smooth clay suitable for the final burnishing of these delightful, engaging figures.

A common thread running through this book shows how often clay objects have been used to service or commemorate the dead. In this and the previous chapter alone there are the sarcophagi of the Etruscans, the memorial to Handel, the heads of Africa celebrating the ancestors and the prehispanic figure found in a tomb shaft. Another theme has been how a scientific and more systematic approach to archaeology has encouraged new, and often still incomplete, discoveries in very recent times.

These two factors are present in the amazing discovery of the underground terracotta army found near Xi'an in the Shaanxi province of China. It is only one part of the mausoleum of Qin Shi Huangdi, who eventually became the first Emperor of China (221–210BC). A replica of the real world,

West Mexico, Nayarit, woman with dog, 15 cm (5 ⅞ in.), pre-Columbian
PHOTOGRAPH © COPYRIGHT THE BRITISH MUSEUM

Opposite and detail:
China, Shaanxi province, first vault of the terracotta army, life-size, 247BC
PHOTO © STEVE DAVEY/LA BELLE AURORE

the building took 36 years to complete and was started in 247BC. It was only discovered in 1974; in 1976 and 1980 there were new finds and excavations still continue.

Serendipity has been noted elsewhere and it was by chance that peasants of the commune, digging a well in an apricot orchard near their village, accidentally came across evidence of a sacrificial tomb. This led to the uncovering of an underground palace so secret that the workmen who had put the treasures in there, were buried alive to ensure that the secret of the entrance died with them. There were also devices triggered to release arrows should any intruder penetrate. It was never intended to be seen by the human eye.

This most spectacular find included more than 7000 life-size models of men and horses. Most of the figures were broken and many appeared to be charred,

but Chinese archaeologists were able to reassemble and place them in precise formation, recognising generals, officers, bowmen and infantrymen by their armour, hair-styles, and positions – a vast military escort to accompany their ruler in death. The skilfully made figures were realistic, not for artistic reason but for practical and religious ones, in the belief that the more life-like they were the more they would be able to fulfil their task of guarding their master in the next world.

Other rulers had been buried with riches such as exquisite jade and bronzes to mark their status; Qin Shi Huangdi marked his in addition by an operation that could only be accomplished by a truly powerful leader with vast resources. A whole army of workers would have been needed to prefabricate the parts and to assemble and colour the figures, to construct and fire the massive and numerous kilns and to gather the formidable quantities of firewood needed for them. The final products were free from flaws, warping or cracking in spite of their size – an average of 2.2 m (6.6 ft.) before firing – taller than the average height in Qin times. Made of a fine textured grey clay, the plentiful loess soil of the North China plain, they were fired to a low earthenware temperature of 950°–1000°C/1742–1832°F.

To simplify such a complex operation of mass production the figure was broken down into components, using a process combining the use of moulds and hand modelling. The moulds were of limited types: two types of legs – hefty enough to support the weight of the figure – and eight types of torsos and heads. By manipulating these and combining them with further prefabricated additions and modelling, a great variety could be achieved, particularly in the detail of hair-styles and facial expressions. The armour was exact and literal and there is little naturalism in the arms and trunk. The hands needed several different moulds for they were holding bronze swords, spears and scimitars which were found unrusted and sharp at the soldiers' feet; any wooden parts have disintegrated although the soldiers' fingers are still curled as though to grasp their weapons.

As in Greek sculptures the army was originally brightly coloured, but now, after 2000 years buried underground, only a few traces of pigment remain. This photograph (*below*), taken of a model in the Museum of Qin Shi Huangdi,

China, Shaanxi province, model – painting the figures, contemporary
PHOTOGRAPH COURTESY OF: PROFESSOR R. MARIAN HICKS, O.B.E.

opened in 1979, gives some indication of the raw brilliance of the colours. They are being ground and mixed and painted flat, with strong colour contrast on the figures, with every part coloured including the face. One officer waits to be painted; he is in monochrome, and it is like this that the reassembled army was first seen. Their role was to defend the Emperor, but they were not alone, for alongside the replica army was a tomb containing real people and real objects to sustain him.

The cavalry horses of the Qin army were fine-bred, short-legged, muscular Chinese ponies from the steppes able to travel long distances at high speed. In the models their tails are plaited and their manes adorned with flowery decorations, the saddles are covered with rows of nail heads and tasseled.

This lively horse (*below*) from the T'ang Dynasty (AD618–907) was of a breed introduced into China from Ferghana in the first century. Larger and more

China, Tang Dynasty, Fhergana horse, 35.7 cm (14 in.), 8th century AD

elegant than the native Chinese pony, with its narrow chest, sinewy build and long legs, it became highly valued – a status symbol for rich and official families. Models of it elaborately caparisoned for war, and of gracefully dressed people and camels, were used as funerary ware.

The Qin method of making figures was adopted by the sculptors of the Han and T'ang Dynasties. The main structure of the horses and camels were made from a number of moulds, so these well known and popular animals of this period appear in fairly set poses, although individual features and ornaments are remarkably varied. This fine example seems to have a vitality that belongs uniquely to itself in the bent neighing head and the impatient pawing of the ground. Although it is only 35.7 cm (14 in.) high it is immensely powerful. This model has worn traces of coloured slip on it, but many were lead-glazed in three main colours – green, amber and cream – a technique known as *sancai*, which came into its own in the 8th century.

These large, polychrome tomb guardians, *(see also p.84)* made in the T'ang Dynasty, are 8th century. They too were made from a variety of moulds with some hand modelling for the details. When completed they were covered with white slip to enhance the brightness of the sancai colours. Here the fluid glaze has been painted on carefully and appropriately to pick out the detail of the armour, but it is frequently splashed on in a more arbitrary way regardless of the form. A common practice was to leave the head, head-dress and hands unglazed as in this example. These celestial guardians, or *fangxiang* figures, were placed in graves, sometimes one in each corner, upholding the popular Buddhist concept of the four Heavenly Kings whose duty it was to guard the four corners of heaven. Fierce and angry, they are dressed for battle each with a wooden sword, long since decayed, in their uplifted hands and crushing underfoot animals usually more terrifying than these mild creatures. Other figures of the spirit world included grotesque animal shapes and exaggerated human forms who stood guard against the evil ones.

China, T'ang Dynasty, tomb guardians, 93.3 cm (36 in.), 8th century AD
PHOTOGRAPH © GLASGOW MUSEUMS, THE BURRELL COLLECTION

Buddhism was introducd into China from the Indian sub-continent early in the Han Dynasty (AD206–220), but ceramic images of its deities are scarcely known before the 13th century. This supremely calm Lohan or disciple *(right)* is of the Ming Dynasty; the sculpture is dated 1484 and it is almost life-size. It is decorated with the T'ang palette of green, cream and amber which is sometimes known as the Ming sancai.

China, Ming Dynasty,
Lohan or disciple, 127 cm
(46 in.), AD1484
PHOTOGRAPH © GLASGOW
MUSEUMS, THE BURRELL
COLLECTION

The simple cut of the robes is discreetly enriched by the ornate flowers on the border, and on the green cloak there are traces of gilt decoration. To achieve the crispness of the border a *cloisonné* process has been used. The edge of the border and the decoration within it have been outlined with a thin slip forming a well. After a first firing the fluxed glazes or enamels are applied within the raised lines before a second firing; with this method there is no fear of the colours mixing.

The modest richness of the robes is matched by the concentrated stillness of the disciple as he sits cross-legged on a stool with his hands at rest in his lap. The unglazed contemplative shaved head, delicately and austerely modelled, pursues its serene meditation.

Clearly this cannot be an account, represented by figures in clay, for all cultures. Some of the many sources not presented include the Haniwa tomb figures and the Jomon cord-patterned figures from Japan, the terracotta figures from Eastern Gujarat in India, and the varied clay sculptures of South American countries. In central Europe the religious tableaux and statues of realistically painted terracotta, so like the polychrome wood-carved versions of the 15th and 16th centuries and the small models, slip-trailed, of medieval England have not been included.

The small faïence or porcelain figures from such well known centres as Meissen, Sèvres, Dresden, Nymphenburg and Capodimonte occupy a further specialist field. They proliferated in the 18th century after a long-sought technical breakthrough. Chinese porcelain – discovered in the 7th century – had long been admired ever since it had come to Europe in the Middle Ages. Although Europeans were keen to copy the style and quality of these wares the material composition of them remained a mystery. After a long and elusive search, success was finally achieved at Meissen, and by the middle of the 18th century porcelain figures and ware were being manufactured throughout Europe.

This English rococo figurine *(right)* is made of English porcelain, a soft paste, which fires at a lower temperature than the more transluscent hard paste, whose secret eluded the English factories. The first and foremost factory using it was founded in Chelsea in 1745 and this figure, dated between 1749–1752, was made soon after. It is one of only three. It represents an Italian actress famed for her beauty and intelligence, Isabella d'Andreini, and was modelled by an artist who dominated design in the Chelsea works, Joseph Willem.

She stands, vacant-faced, attached to her low plinth, dressed elaborately but modestly in a gown made of a rich flower-decorated fabric with full sleeves and skirt. With one elegant hand she raises her skirt and reveals a yellow underslip; she wears a red lace-edged bustier and blue shoes. The enamel colours are hand-painted. The main concentration of interest on what must have been a luxury item is the costume of this small decorative figure.

Finally, here is a figure similar in scale *(see overleaf)*, made 34 centuries earlier, in the 16th century BC. Unlike Isabella, it is not wholly decorative but is a votive object. It is Minoan, from the non-Greek island of Crete. It is made of

England, Chelsea, Rococo
figurine, 24.1 cm (9 ½ in.),
c.1749–1752

Crete, Minoan, Snake
Goddess, 29.5 cm
(11 ⅝ in.); 16th century BC
PHOTOGRAPH © ASHMOLEAN
MUSEUM, UNIVERSITY OF
OXFORD

6
The Figure in Contemporary Ceramics

I have written elsewhere (*Coiled Pottery – Traditional and Contemporary Ways*) that 'the contemporary potter is armed with explicit technical information about clay and its behaviour, about firing methods, pigments and colouring agents and can consciously select what, how and why he makes.' Potters need to find their own symbols and meanings outside the needs of community, ritual or firm, continuing traditions or skills.

Recently many have used the human figure as a vehicle for channelling their experiences. Some artists have looked back to past civilisations, many have focused on their own emotions, while others have started from an aesthetic formality or from a process; occasionally a political agenda has been explored or an attitude to contemporary society expressed. Even in the past when tied to a functional purpose, the human head and figure have borne sentiments of dignity, of humour, of pathos, of *joie de vivre*, of satire, of sexual celebration, of horror and tragedy. The deep, underlying factors of being human mean that these common characteristics are also found in the work of the potter today even though their context, fashion and concerns may be very different.

We have seen how artists are circumscribed and stimulated by the culture and time in which they live and how some works actually come to define a period in the imagination. Two notable potters whose work is representative of the different eras in which they studied are R.J. Washington and William Newland, although only separated by birth by six years, the first born in 1913, the second in 1919. They died within a year of each other in 1997 and 1998 respectively. Both studied painting in art school before becoming involved in clay in their teacher-training year. Washington did a post-graduate year at the Royal College of Art from 1937–8, while William Newland did his teacher-training at London University Institute of Education from 1947–8. Only ten years distanced their

Opposite:
Claire Curneen *Blue Series II,* approx. 35 cm (13 ¾ in.), 2000
PHOTOGRAPH COURTESY OF THE ARTIST

103

R.J. Washington *Mother and Child, approx.* 37.5 cm (14 ¾ in.), 1980–81

initial introduction to ceramics yet the style of their work and the attitude they brought to it were totally different due, I suggest, largely to ethos rather than to temperament.

This pot thrown by R.J. Washington, like the one pictured by him in Chapter Two, was made in 1980, yet it has many of the characteristics and strictures encouraged by his teacher, the potter William Staite Murray, who taught at the Royal College of Art from 1926–1939. The intrusion of World War II and his subsequent work as an Inspector of Art meant that Washington potted little and exhibited less for many years; it was not until 1979 that he was able to return to full-time potting, and when he did so he resumed where he had left off.

Those features that are reminiscent of the pre-war ceramic school of the Royal College of Art are the tall anthropomorphic shape of the bottle form, the pronounced throwing rings, the turned foot and the emphasis on texture rather than colour. Washington was very aware of the inherent sculptural qualities of the pot and had inherited the idea of pottery as an art form equal to painting, so gave titles to his figuratively painted works – this one is called *Mother and Child*. Subsequently he made richly coloured platters, but it is essentially his tall, figurative painted pots, redolent of the pre-war years, for which he is best known

Unlike R.J. Washington, William Newland, a New Zealander, had lived an adventurous and colourful life before he went to art school. He joined the New Zealand Expeditionary Force when World War II broke out and served in Greece and the Middle East before becoming a prisoner-of-war in Germany and Italy. He arrived in London in the 1940s and studied painting at Chelsea School of Art, but it was while training as a teacher that he discovered his affinity with clay at London University's Institute of Education, and it was in the basement pottery there that he remained for the whole of his influential teaching career. Like Washington he became a dedicated art educator, but he was abe to continue potting. It was Dora Billington at the Central School of Arts and Crafts to whom Washington turned for technical advice when he was a student, and it was she who later initiated Newland into the technique of tin glazing and the bright colours it could call out. It was not only an antidote to the prevalent sombre neoclassical stoneware, but echoed Picasso's lighthearted ceramics which he made during the war at Vallauris. They were seen for the first time in England in 1950. They stimulated, by their novelty, the new surge of energy created by the rich optimism of peace when, as Newland recalled 'everyone was full of enthusi-asm . . . we thought that we were going to change the world'. As far as style was concerned there was indeed a change of mood in architecture and design of all kinds exemplified by the gaiety of the Festival of Britain. Coffee bars were open-ing in Central London and were smart places to meet while there was still aus-terity. They too presented a brave new face; many of them were lightheartedly decorated by ceramic sculptures made by Newland and his future wife Margaret Hine, of figurative groups of Minoan bulls, harlequins, fishermen, women releasing doves or seated on donkeys. Strong in invention, visually bold and highly decorative they helped to capture the spirit of the Festival style with their fusion of eclectic garnerings from the past and skills of the present.

The elitist fine art attitude of the inter-war years was exchanged for a more widely spread, populist, accessible appeal.

The peg-shaped figure of a woman (*below*) carrying grapes bears a strong resemblance to another on a donkey; William Newland made several figurative

William Newland *Horse and Rider*, dish, ht. approx. 51 cm (20 in.), contemporary
PHOTOGRAPH BY SHEILA PAINE, COURTESY OF: NEWLAND ESTATE.

Eric Mellon, *Circus Horse and Rider,* dish, approx. 28 cm (11 in.), 1970

groups of the *Flight into Egypt*, including a mother with a child on her lap, seated sideways in the same way, on a similar donkey. Staffordshire figures from the 19th century as well as something of Picasso were two potent influences evident in his work.

Opposite:
Mo Jupp, Red Form, 30 cm (11 ¾ in.), 1999

In many ways the subject matter of the post-war years, the nymphs, fauns and satyrs of Picasso, the Mediterranean brightness of Newland's work might seem to be carried on by Eric Mellon in his *Circus* paintings of the late 1960s; yet the subject matter of his work, with its symbolism, often autobiographical, is deeply personal to him. He works through transmutation, using myth and folk lore. The circus horse of 1969 later becomes Pluto's horses; the trapeze artists, placing faith in each other in an act that could lead to disappointment and tragedy, become lovers in a later work, and embrace. Daphne changes into a tree in the myth of Daphne and Apollo, while later exchanging the leaves on her outstretched arms for feathers, she becomes a bird maiden and eventually changes into an angel. Each painting, complete in itself, is a continuation of his own romantic imagination.

Mo Jupp has concentrated almost entirely on the female figure for many years; before that, in the early 1960s, he had been making a huge variety of experimental hand-built works. The subject of the female which has occupied him since 1978 has remained fairly constant and he is always looking for better ways to say what he means in the way he uses clay to express his re-focused attitudes. He can manipulate clay with experienced ease, using traditional hollow pottery techniques, and is influenced by a wide diversity of cross-cultural references and a feeling for the archaic. The scale of his work ranges from 10 cm (4 in.) to life-size or more.

In the typical examples from 1996 and 1999 (*right and overleaf*) Jupp has built thick-legged, wide-hipped women with slim waists and torsos and small, neat breasts. His forms are frequently cut off at the knees, although sometimes feet and legs emerge attached to their clay plinths; they are headless and armless, the concentration homing in on their sexual attributes. Sometimes, although not in these images, the upper body may be somewhat abstracted by becoming a flattened curve like a neck or an elephant's trunk, or the neck may be broken off irregularly; generally the hips and buttocks are clearly defined. On occasions a pleated sarong emphasises the provocative hollow-backed poses with hips swaying to one side. In the earlier grey figure we can see the fresh way in which a slab has been used to build the shoulders and indicate the neck. In the red form, treated with white slip,

Mo Jupp, *Grey Form*, 0.6 m
(2 ft) 1996

PHOTOGRAPH COURTESY OF
PETER'S BARN GALLERY

there is a contrast between the sturdy legs and the gracefully flexed back. Larger works are made in sections: a full-sized figure may require five pieces.

His iconography is female, however abstract and strangely proportioned, although he is stretching the imagination to its ultimate point of recognition in the rod sculptures. He calls the thin 2 m (6 ft) tall rod-supported shapes 'female icons'. They bear only the most minimal reference to their subject by the minute shell-like breasts which are set very close together and scarcely discernible, as these ceramic rods divide the world vertically. The hollow clay tubes, threaded on the rigid metal like beads, are as neutral and austere as his other pieces are voluptuous and intimate.

In the 1970s potters made pots and there was little interest in what could be described as the fine art approach of those who had ambition to be seen as sculptors; they found themselves in the invidious position of neither fitting into the world of ceramics nor of fine art. Interest grew in figurative sculptural ceramics in the 1980s, encouraged by a move away from abstract art by painters in America and Britain and the liberating and expressive possibilities opened up by hand-building. Although it is still not always easy to place such work, it has become an acceptable genre of expression in which lies some of the most interesting and inventive work of today.

One of the first sculptors who worked in ceramics to be represented uniquely by a fine art gallery was Glenys Barton (born 1944) – a figurative artist from the early 1970s. Her early work was cast in bone china and finished by hand – a

Above, left:
Mo Jupp, female icons,
2m (6 ft), 1997
PHOTOGRAPH COURTESY OF:
PETER'S BARN GALLERY

Above, right:
Mo Jupp, female icon,
2m (6 ft), 1997
PHOTOGRAPH COURTESY OF:
PETER'S BARN GALLERY

Glenys Barton *Jean Muir*,
67 cm (27 in.), 1992

technique which, already expertly mastered, was extended in 1976 when she became artist-in-residence at Wedgwood in Staffordshire. Here every modern facility in the factory was available to her, including the opportunity to collaborate by designing pieces which were produced in limited editions for Wedgwood.

Working on the human figure since 1974, Barton's early works included small figures set on plaques of bone china and large cast heads, often with screen-printed decoration. These were impersonal, neutral, emblematic figures which represented humanity in a most general way – universal rather than individual man.

In December 1977 she took stock of her work declaring: 'Drawing from life is the only activity that I am allowing myself as I feel that it will take me back to essential and basic considerations'. The drawing she pursued was not illustrative but a means of searching out a more abstract level of thinking which would be useful to her as a sculptor. Out of this came a series of heads of friends who had modelled for her; they were not likenesses or portraits, but austerely beautiful images with shaven heads and expressionless faces. Later, in order to express the individuality of a person she emphasised their distinguishing features, slip-casting and hand-building one-off pieces which were sometimes smoke-fired. Working from photographs she began to coil heads, producing several sculptures of each, until she recognised in one the distillation of the image she was after.

While working on the sculpture *(left)* of the fashion designer, Jean Muir, of 1992, she also made several small figures of her cast in fine earthenware-slip as well as a group of modelled heads. These portraits were whole or three-quarter length bodies, heads and shoulders or just faces. The head is modelled and left uncoloured, in others the modelled head may be coloured or the features may be painted on. Hands had long fascinated her and were made as independent sculptures; they play an important part in this figure where the gesture is significant in a sculpture of such overt simplicity and where the cut of the hair, the angle of the shoulders, the slight twist of the body and the tailoring of the garment as well as the position of arms, hands and feet all play a clear and unambiguous

role in a deceptively complex sculpture made with delicate precision and sureness.

The bald, boulder-like heads of this sculpture called *Listen*, made in 1997, share in silence sounds which may or may not be there, for they have no ears! They doze with eyes shut or wait patiently, impassive. This hand-built piece, coiled and modelled, consists of two U-shaped forms that relate to each other, blue profile confronting blue profile, not quite touching, each of them consisting of four interlocked heads unaware that they are existing in the same shell. They share the timeless quality for which Glenys Barton aims.

Initially Glenys Barton used bone china because it was such a satisfying and beautiful material with which to carry out her ideas, but it restricted the scale in which she could build, so she changed to a fine earthenware clay.

Christie Brown press-moulds her figures (*overleaf*), which are close to life-size, using soft slabs of a much coarser clay, either red from reclaimed unfired house bricks or T-material, which is white. Although she started using moulds – cast in plaster from a coiled model – as a technical device, it has now developed into an intrinsic part of the process. She uses large fragments of rolled clay laid in the mould, making no attempt to disguise the seams, which are formed where they join, but rather emphasising them by painting. (It was Rodin who first drew attention to the sculptural process by leaving the seams of his moulds unchased,

Glenys Barton *Listen*, 41 x 67 x 29 cm (16 x 26 ⅛ x 11 ½ in.), 1997

PHOTOGRAPH COURTESY OF: FLOWERS EAST GALLERY, LONDON, © COPYRIGHT ADRIAN FLOWERS

Christie Brown *Olympia's Helper,* 110 cm (44 in.), 1999

PHOTOGRAPH BY KATE FORREST, COURTESY OF THE ARTIST

imprinted on the plaster or bronze cast.) The method allows for replication; she is able to work in groups that can be repeated several times. A short series where the figures were pressed from the same mould was called *Clone,* while another theme was *Twins.* It also allows for a certain amount of variety. The stance of the bodies, the angle to which a head is joined to the body, the position of an arm, or the character of the facial features can be altered. These are all measures which were used in creating the Chinese Army. Other variations are due to the condition of the clay when it is pressed into the mould, and the slips and engobes which are applied before a second firing.

Her ideas have been inspired by the life drawing that she has always enjoyed. Her first figures were free-standing headless torsos, slab-built with a little low relief; she was in a sense giving her drawing a back and a front and standing it upright. She started her moulded figures in 1995 with a series called the *Cast of Characters,* also torsos without arms, but now three-dimensional and with the strangely withdrawn inward-looking heads which also characterise her later full length figures.

Christie Brown has always been alive to a great many sources – abstract ideas such as attachment and loss found in the *Cast of Characters,* mythology and visual historical references which include echoes of Classical sculpture such as pre-Hellenic Kouroi and Etruscan sculpture of the archaic period. Her latest work is informed by the ritual uses of ceramic as grave sculpture such as the Chinese terracotta army or the archaic Egyptian grave helpers (Shabti) and makes use of various creation myths like that of Prometheus, the creator and Galatea, the creation.

Olympia's Helper stands grounded on thick legs reminiscent of the warriors of the Chinese army, and with her arms complete, seems almost capable of movement. She looks straight ahead with undeviating eyes. This sculpture is stacked in clearly defined sections; for public showing it will be reinforced with an armature.

Moller's Golem, 168 cm (67 in.) high, stands firmly on feet and legs and has the same pallid, other-worldly look as the *Helper* and although he too looks as

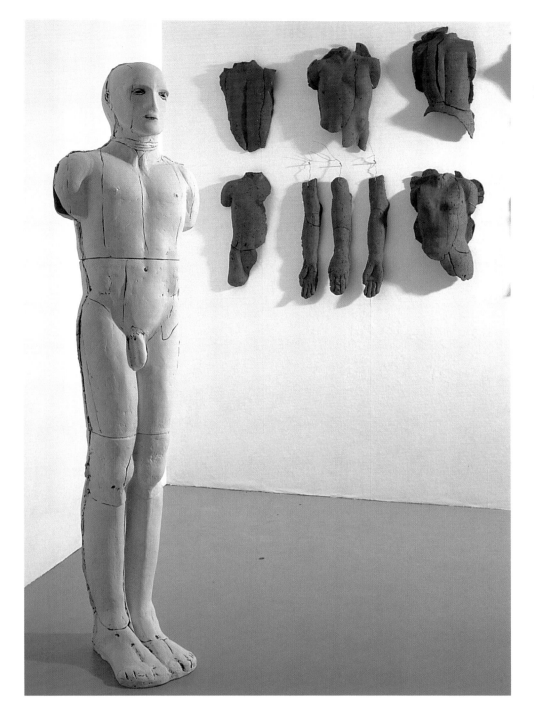

Christie Brown, *Møller's Golem,* 168 cm (67 in.), 1998–9

Photograph by Kate Forrest, courtesy of the artist

though he is about to stride forward is still an embodiment of passivity. Behind, in a separate group, are a number of body parts made in coarse clay brick, *Ex Votos*, which harness the power of the gods to heal and soothe. With their staring eyes and their exraordinary pallor these two figures appear to have risen from the dead; indeed, as wet, floppy slabs of clay they have been laid tomb-like

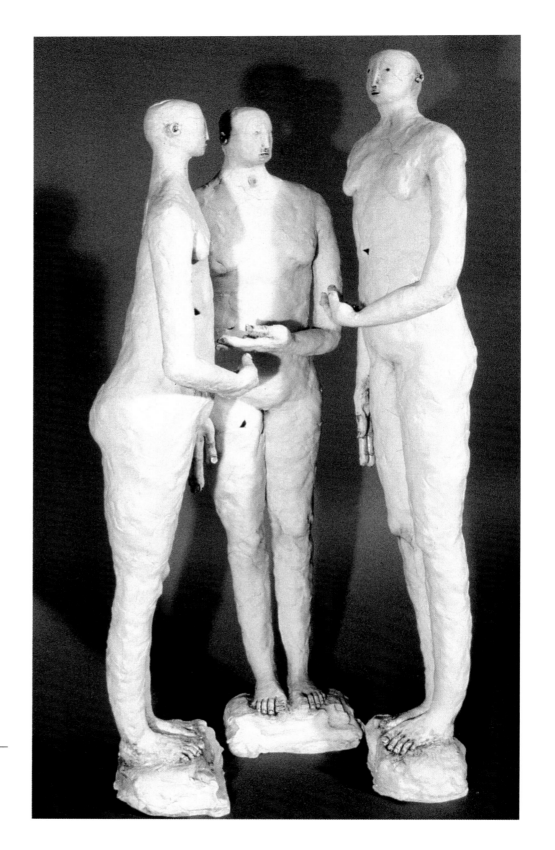

Claire Curneen, *Standing Figures*, tallest: 63 cm (24 ¾ in.), 1998

Photograph courtesy of the artist

in their mould, to dry and shrink and remain forever in the poses assigned to them.

Christie Brown has found inspiration from the past for both form and content, but it is combined with a more personal and contemporary dilemma which she describes as a concern with 'the expression of certain subjective ideas and vague intuitive apprehension which it is difficult to define.'

It is tempting, and perhaps correct, to think that the way Claire Curneen builds her figures (left) describes their poignant presences. The thin clay walls randomly built and the small accidental holes revealing the dark hollow interior seem to parallel the fragile distraught angst of the enquiring, purposeless gaze of the figures and the emptiness of their inner secrets. The fragility of human flesh and skin is suggested incidentally by the way the figures are built up with small patches of pinched clay lightly meeting or joined together; where two pieces fail to meet small fissures or holes are formed. These are not anatomic studies; long thin dangling arms, diminutive hairless heads and extra large hands create a personal language of proportions that somehow turns these otherwise depersonalised characters into vulnerable individuals.

They are individuals who look out at the world with raisin-like eyes; they often stand together but rarely interact. In this group of figures, however, there does seem to be something going on as the two shorter figures look to the third one expectantly – perhaps to pronounce, elucidate, explain, prophesy, or reassure. Is she a teacher, a prophet, a holy person? We do not know the story but are caught by the possibilities. Claire Curneen has said: 'Looking at early Italian Renaissance paintings, like those of Piero della Francesca or Masaccio, there is always an obvious story or narration. My figures give a hint or suggestion of a story or of a happening.'

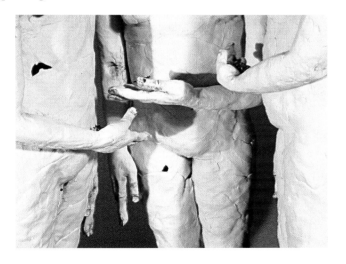

Claire Curneen,
detail of hands

The detail shows how actively the hands communicate. As in the work of Glenys Barton, hands play an important part in the sculptures – not gentle, soft, elegant hands, but large bony long-fingered ones often dangling helplessly by the side of the figure, modelled in great detail like the tiny feet.

It is not immediately apparent that these are women; their bulky bodies lack curves but they do undoubtedly have small high sagging breasts. These androgynous creatures are ageless but the drooping breasts, the shapeless forms and the dimpled nature of their skin suggest that they are not very young. In these naked figures she has almost eliminated the idea of gender, preferring to illustrate a human rather than a feminine theme. Yet the images do touch on her own emotional experiences and relationships and it is in confronting personal concerns that she reveals universal anxieties.

In her most recent work Curneen has moved away from the dry unglazed, colourless surface; now, on shiny, clear glaze the figure is clothed in a tattoo-like blue-flowered transfer (*see p.102*). It is as if the flowers were growing all over the body or emerging, flowing from it, spilling over the base on which the torso rests – flowers beautiful but short-lived, a symbol of life and death. The small fissures and holes are not part of the surface now although the figure is built up in the same way and the pressed sections of clay still faintly map the skin. These figures are not large: they are approximtely 34 cm (13 ½ in.) high.

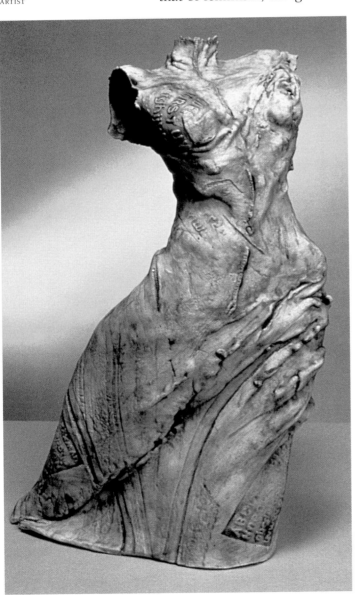

Tracey Heyes, *Grecian*, 52 cm (21 in.), 1993
PHOTOGRAPH COURTESY OF THE ARTIST

Tracey Heyes has used her sculpture to tackle contemporary issues, particularly that of feminism, using the metaphor of dress. She has made sculpture of delicate belts, bodices and corsets not only to show sexuality but also to illustrate the constraints – physical, emotional and social – that women have been exposed to throughout history. The rigidity caused by the tightening of laces, bones and zips to enhance the figure has sometimes been represented by her, in clay, as armour or metallic relics from antiquity. She is aware of the difference between how women feel and how they appear, and knows that the often inhibiting restrictions of fashion not only disguise but also reveal the desirable shape of woman.

This 52 cm (21 in.) high sculpture of 1993 is called *Grecian*. The unclothed figure is clearly delineated under the folds and drapes of the dress as in the Greek sculpture on p.72. Unlike the Greek male, who is generally portrayed nude, she is both clothed and revealed. But is this a figure or only a suggestion of one? The emphatic hollowness of the form suggests that the dress and the person are indistinguishable.

The way Tracey Heyes manipulates the clay has been influenced by the enjoyment she took in sewing from a young age, and particularly in the cutting of the paper-thin patterns. In her ceramic the dress is constructed in hand-built slabs which are rolled and impressed before they are cut and assembled. Once constructed the clay is then thinned by pushing it from the inside outward to give the quality of dry skin or fabric.

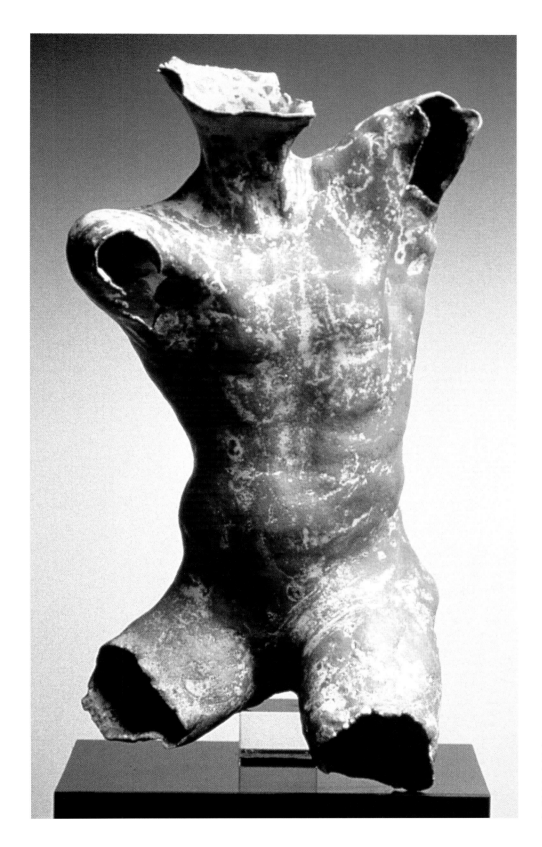

Helen Ridehalgh, *Male
Torso*, 64 cm (26 in.),
1995–6
PHOTOGRAPH COURTESY OF THE
ARTIST

Helen Ridehalgh, *Female Torso*, 64 cm (26 in.), 1994

PHOTOGRAPH COURTESY OF THE ARTIST

Other sculptors have been directly affected by Classical art. Helen Ridehalgh has experienced wide-ranging influences, from prehistoric European, to that of Italian and Classical Greek sculpture as well as the forms of pre-Columbian terracotta figures. However, the over-riding influence on her work for more than a decade has been the power and energy she recognised in a small fired *bozzetto* by Michelangelo, called *Atlas Slave* which was made in 1527.

Most of the artists described in this chapter come from a craft-based background, but Helen Ridehalgh studied in a fine art department using traditional sculpture methods, and this has somewhat dictated the way she works and her attitude to the figure. She starts by making a study in clay modelled directly from life – a *bozzetto* – carefully choosing the model and the pose.

The sculpture is then built with small, thin strips of clay – particularly evident in the thighs of the female figure (*left*) – into the final hollow form. She uses T-material which gives her the flexibility to push and pull the pose from inside and outside until she is satisfied that a distillation of the energy and muscle rhythms of the body, which she has already captured in the immediacy of the initial clay sketch, have been achieved. The approximate scale of her figures is 64 cm (26 in.).

The surface colour that she requires comes largely from her experience of metal-working techniques, particularly bronze casting. The whiteness of the clay acts as a canvas on which she can create the patination of ageing metals by using washes of colour, combining underglaze oxides with an alkaline glaze, which she sprays on and rubs back several times. The work is fired to 1250°C/2282°F in an oxidising atmosphere.

Like the particular example by Tracey Heyes, her sculptures are overtly hollow torsos but her motivation lies in the classical ideal of the beauty of the living body, and her own experience of the inner reality she reads into it.

The work of Ruth Barrett-Danes (*overleaf*) is small in scale and intimate; it explores a strange narrative world of active and often uncomfortable relationships estranged from everyday experiences. Her influences lie outside ceramics and are rooted in the fantasies of such artists as Arthur Rackham, Hieronymus Bosch, Pieter Breughel, the bestiaries and Romanesque sculpture. Deeply human ambiguities of personality are disguised by the use of animal-headed figures; these figures may be descendants of the symbolic animals found in the Mardi Gras, but they are not masked. With their shiny, popping aggressive eyes they have a ferocious reality – creatures of nightmares. Initially engulfed in thrown forms the figures, often reptilian, struggle to emerge or be born. Later they were modelled onto bases which were coiled or moulded, allowing a greater flexibility of expression. The figures are built by a pinch-coiled method. Porcelain suits the scale and produces a high degree of definition, while its qualities in the making and the final coldness in handling suit the subject matter. Sometimes a stained porcelain is used, polished to reveal the embedded colour; or, to get a different surface interest, *terra sigillata* may be added or a vitreous slip may be

sprayed on and rubbed back. Many pieces are fired four times – biscuit at 1000°C/1832°F, a second and if necessary further adjustments, at 1200°C/2192°F and finally, a lower firing for the lustre which is often used for those gleaming eyes.

This group *(above)* is made of burnished porcelain; the only glaze was used for the lustred eyes. There is something of the reptile in these beak-headed crea-

120

Ruth Barrett-Danes, *It Takes Two to Tango*, 45 cm (18 in.), 1997

PHOTOGRAPH COURTESY OF THE ARTIST

tures. Are they in complicity as they join hands, or are they predators battling for position on the back of the ovoid-shaped animal which they ignore? The answer, perhaps, is to be found in the title – *Three's a Crowd*.

These two happy creatures of 1997 are made of stained porcelain. A more joyful and abandoned mood emerges with the rhythms of the dance in *It Takes*

Two to Tango as these two liberated personalities sway their heavy, awkward bodies on small flexed feet in an improbably lighthearted duet.

Michael Flynn painted for ten years before studying ceramics at Cardiff College of Art where he met the Barrett-Danes, Alan who taught there and Ruth, whose work he found exciting. Although he and Ruth make small modelled figures their work and sources are quite different. While her work is devoid of superficial tactile qualities, his owes much to the character of wet clay quickly modelled. Her work is inspired by macabre visual material and is highly personal; his ideas and observations were brought together and formulated through literature, particularly 19th-century romantic writings from Germany and middle Europe, and is explosive and outward-looking. Visually he is stimulated by the exuberance of Latin America or Spanish religious art and the German expressionists.

Rodin and Bourdelle are two sculptors he admires; following them, his large stoneware pieces preserve the energetic marks of process with no deliberate attempt to finish or polish. Fascination with ceramic process and sculptural considerations has led to work in a variety of scales and the use of a number of clay

Michael Flynn, *The Ship of Fools*, 56 cm (22 in.), 1997

bodies, ranging from heavily grogged figures, often raku-fired in stoneware, to modelled figurines in porcelain. In spite of occasional life-size figures he intends that his work be considered as domestic icons.

The Ship of Fools is one of a series where writhing figures clamber over each other in a small aimless ship *(left)*. This piece, in salt-glazed porcelain, has all the decorative activity of the rococo. The clay has been squeezed and pushed into a triangular shape where gesture and purpose are described in an overall image of feverish action and where some characters are seen anxiously alert while others are oblivious to their situation.

Catching the Cock has been another recurring theme. It is a subject that has a

Michael Flynn, *Catching the Cock*, 36 cm (14 in.), 1999
PHOTOGRAPH COURTESY OF:
CONTEMPORARY APPLIED ARTS

multitude of references, as the cock occupies a powerful place in folklore, myth and psychology; it features in the prelude to the Crucifixion and is a symbol of vigilance and resurrection. All these references are there to be interpreted by the viewer, or the image can be taken as it is.

This example of his work combines an interest in dance and drama with an admiration for the Meissen tradition, where often the earthy clownishness and sexual elements of the subject matter are contrasted with the refinement of the glazed porcelain. The Pan-like male nude, with flowers wreathed round his head, leaps to catch the protesting cock, an action which brings his limbs into a graceful configuration as he stretches one bent leg.

Pamela Leung, *Fish Figure Fountain*, 81 cm x 60 cm (32 in. x 23 ½ in.), 1992
PHOTOGRAPH COURTESY OF THE ARTIST

Opposite:
Pamela Leung, *Handstand Monkey,* 120 cm (48 in.), 1999
PHOTOGRAPH COURTESY OF THE ARTIST

The figures made by Pamela Leung, like those of Ruth Barrett-Danes, are animal-headed. For her they are a vehicle for expressing attitudes which are both symbolic and real. She is of Chinese descent and spent the first 14 years of her life in Hong Kong; many of her references have been taken from Chinese mythology. Her half-animal, half-human forms arose from the ancient Chinese belief that sacred animals have the ability to change into human form, and that deities are equally respected both as human and animal. Animals can also change into demons, symbolising the idea that humanity, however civilised, can be tainted by the forces of evil. Her personal, surreal, dreamlike work has evolved from a world where myth and reality co-exist and from an acceptance that the strange is normal. It is from her happy childhood world – and particularly memories of the brightly painted, gruesome, concrete grottoes of Tiger Bahn park in Hong Kong – that she funds her ideas. She says that it was by coming to the West that she is able to draw so clearly on the ever-fresh, unchanging memories of her youth.

This fish-headed figure (left) sits in a basin shaped like a scallop shell and drinks the water that gushes from the palms of his hands; it is a fountain, made in two pieces to allow for the pump in the middle. Her animals are mystical creatures made in familiar form and during the making her ideas may change or resonances from other sources may creep in; for example, the basin recalled to her the Botticelli painting of Venus arising.

The monkey is a later piece, made in two pieces as it is 120 cm (48 in.) high. It is technically a feat to make a figure in movement, balanced on its hands to this scale, and the technique was a major force for her during its making. Her work is mainly coiled using a grogged body – crank mixture – and fired between 1160°–1200°C/2120°–2192°F. During the making and the firing the work has to be supported with kiln stilts or props to prevent distortion; the hands and arms of the monkey, for example, could easily sag in the kiln. The image combines the Oriental love of acrobats with the

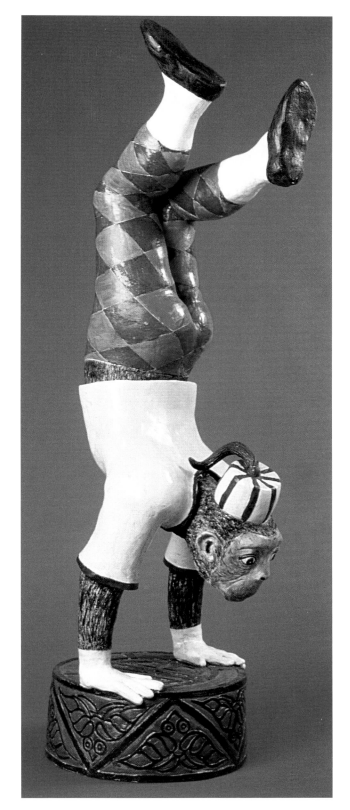

importance of the clever monkey-god in Chinese myth. As in all her work the Chinese influence extends to the bold use of colour; in this case the strong red on the striped legs is achieved by a red glaze with an extra final firing using an enamel glaze.

Rosa Nguyen's Eurasian background has a strong influence on her work despite the fact that she was brought up in the UK. She has travelled widely but did not visit Vietnam, her father's birthplace, until 1991.

She has a direct and unsentimental approach to her animal sculpture which derives from the Buddhist traditions of her family and her own far-flung travels, rather than from legend or myth. She respects the everyday reality of life and death in a matter-of-fact way which fits in with Buddhist ideas. Sacrificial goats, the sacred cows of India and Spanish bulls have all featured among her subjects and other animals include elephants, monkeys and sheep. Many of her sculptures approach life-size and some are raku-fired. She spends much time drawing at the Natural History Museum in London, as this allows her to become familiar with the characteristics of animals before she commits them to clay.

At one time Nguyen concentrated on drawing the horse and in this sculpture

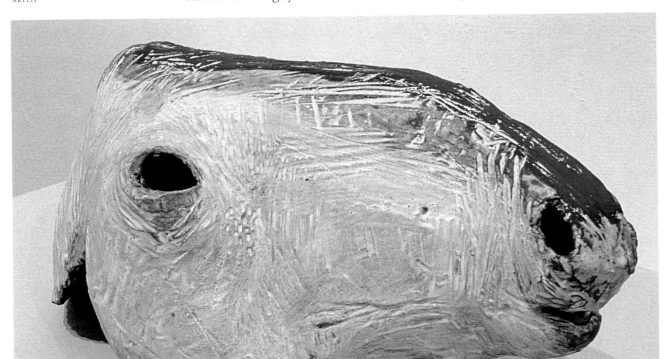

Rosa Nguyen *Horse's Head,* ht. 40 cm (16 in.), 1995

of 1995, 40 cm (16 in.) high, she displays her own feeling for the beast, its essence expressed through the tradition of hand-building in clay. It is interesting to compare this personal response with the head from Taranto (*see p. 75*) and the Chinese T'ang horse (*p. 95*).

Rosa Nguyen, *Red Cow, White Cow*, approx. life-size, 1993

Her animals are open underneath and their undisguised inner volume is explored in the hollow eye sockets and nostrils. She starts from the head with a pinch pot for the nose which she enlarges with coils. She supports the larger pieces with props of wood and rolled-up newspapers.

A wooden slat is employed to beat the head or body into shape, its marks are left to add to the textured energy of the piece, and are clearly seen following the form of these life-size animals (*above*). The grey-bodied clay has been coloured with a white slip, while the lively creature at the back has been painted with a red slip.

Animals also feature strongly in the work of Anna Lambert, an expert modeller, who, unlike other artists mentioned in this chapter, makes things which are to be used domestically. She hand-builds eggcups, cups and saucers, jugs, teapots and bowls – things that are normally thrown in repetition production ware – and decorates them with images of witty and light-hearted birds, fish and land-scapes, in a form of rustic story-telling.

In Chapter 2 we saw plates which were decorated with modelling and relief. Anna Lambert has treated some of her platters in this way – fish swim in a rip-

ple-rimmed dish, modelled birds fly over a field lined by tracks made by a trac-
tor, a variety of painted fish, each recognisable, swim within a wide fish-
embossed rim.

These low-relief dishes have almost been replaced by pots which have become
figures, largely of animals. This knowing-eyed cockerel (*opposite*) is complete as
a decorative object but the upper part of the body can be removed and becomes
a lid for a soup tureen, while the topmost feather of the splendid tail is the neat
handle of the eminently practical ladle.

Her pieces start as pinch pots which are added to, three coils at a time, and
then scraped. The modelling is done after the dampened form is wrapped and
left for a while. After a biscuit firing of 1085°C/1985°F each piece is covered
with a matt black glaze which is washed off, darkening the grooves and scratch-
es to emphasise the texture and unify the form. Underglaze colours, stains and
oxides mixed with gum arabic are painted on the body and finally the pieces are
dipped or sprayed with a clear glaze before a final firing.

Opposite:
Anna Lambert, cockerel
tureen, 28 cm (11 in.),
contemporary

Above:
Anna Lambert, cockerel
tureen with lid removed
PHOTOGRAPHS COURTESY OF THE
ARTIST

Sandy Brown makes domestic pieces as well as sculpture. In general her
ware is not figurative but occasionally one of her freely modelled forms may
'leap' onto the lid of a thrown teapot, its formless arms like wings, triumphantly
extended (*see above*).

In her sculptures a recurring theme is the earth goddess, celebrating the state
of being a woman and her own changing awareness of it. She admits that, whatever her intention, the figures she makes are herself and that in making them
they reflect and anticipate her own personal growth. The thread running
through Brown's work has been both narrative and commentary, with even an
element of exorcism. A recurring nightmare of not being able to fly, for example,
stopped when she made a sculpture called the *Bird God*. Constant subjects are
gods, goddesses, demons, lovers and mythological creatures.

Sandy Brown's recent work includes some larger than life-size figures; this
woman with two butterflies fluttering on her outstretched hand (*right*) is over

Sandy Brown, *Woman with Two Butterflies*, 210 cm (84 in.), contemporary

Photograph courtesy of the artist

Christy Keeney, *Standing Square Man*, 37 cm (14 ½ in.), 2000

210 cm (83 in.) high. The clay is strengthened with glass fibre to hold the weight of the coiled forms during the drying and firing. Her dishes are covered with rich and casual-seeming painting and something of this spontaneity is evident in this painted figure. Although the circles and whirls follow the body forms there is a slap-happy freedom with which the marks are placed on this womanly Amazon-like figure which belies the instinctive appropriateness and confidence which is the result of assured experience.

Uninhibited in her own life and femininity she is also very unconstrained in the way she works, which is direct and is left, unfussily, in the way it comes out.

Christy Keeney makes figures that stand up in space three-dimensionally, yet with a strong two-dimensional character. Seen from the narrow side they display the method of making: in slab-moulded forms, like a double-sided plaque and are similar to cut-out drawings standing up, silhouettes with a picture on the back and the front. They are press-moulded from a two-piece mould cast from a solid carved block, and the basic cast shapes are modified by additions, particularly of hair and ears and sometimes arms. Mask-like flat, ovalled faces are drawn into the clay or built up.

Christy Keeney, *Standing Woman,* 37 cm x 10 cm (14 ½ in. x 4 in.), 2000
PHOTOGRAPH COURTESY OF THE ARTIST

At one time Keeney made portrait sculpture to commission so these flat heads and figures, part drawing, part sculpture, were a deliberate move toward finding a more personal and flexible attitude to clay and the human form.

The *Standing Square Man* has a rich textural surface. The earthy weathered appearance is achieved by a slurry of soft clay painted over the crank mixture which is used to build the main structure, followed by soft washes of colour. The deliberate incisions of the drawing and any other incidental marks are highlighted by the manganese and copper which are rubbed in after the first firing and before the painting of other oxides and underglaze colours.

This standing woman is a more complicated image. One horizontal arm clutches her far shoulder, crossing the semi-circle formed by the neck and the lower arm which sweeps across the body. The placing of the neck and head create a curious ambiguity of viewpoint, as the woman seems to be seen from both the front and side view. The painting of the dress with the two circles which may represent breasts is somewhat reminiscent of the Mycenean idol in Chapter 1.

These two heads *(above)*, 41 cm (16 in.) high and 17 cm (6 ¾ in.) deep, are made from the same mould. It is the painting of the hair and the area surrounding the face and neck which allows for individuality, for example the position and shape of the heads. Here the coarse crank mixture used in the making is covered with a fine white, smooth, earthenware slip and it is into this that the features have been scratched , with the typically small, widespread eyes close to the hair-line, the long straight-nostrilled nose and the small pursed mouth.

In his recent work Richard Slee creates a whole environment in which to place his figures. They exist in a world that has evolved through a variety of surprising and unfashionable influences that have coalesced in his highly personal capricious and witty creations. His enthusiasms include the earthenware of 18th century Staffordshire and Victorian art pottery, the freshness of the decorated colour in Sèvres porcelain, the suburban ornaments of middle-class England, things

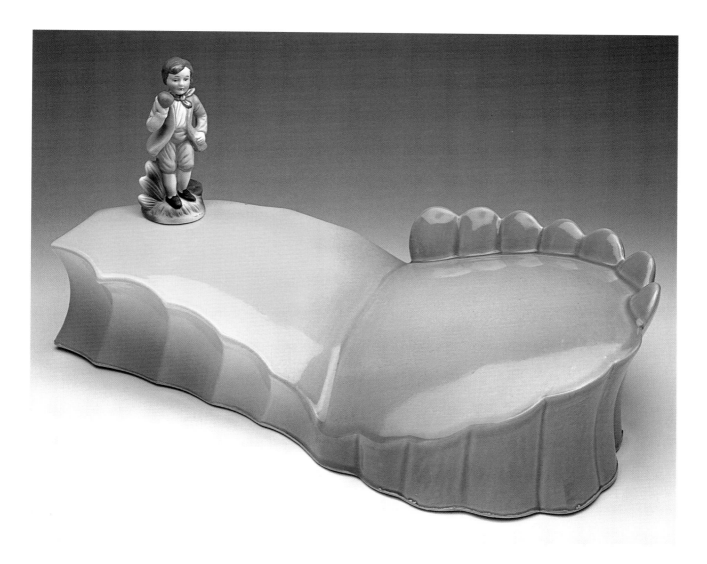

which are nationalistic and uniquely English such as the toby jug or Punch and Judy puppet figures, as well as toys, commemoration objects and trophies. Pottery with shiny glazes in primary and pastel colours pared down for mass production are also part of this nostalgia for the cheap and cheerful. He is also drawn to the surrealists and by certain popular cartoon drawings.

Whether he is handbuilding cornucopias, flowers, flasks or fronds, tankards or toby jugs his ideas are worked with impeccable technique and craftsmanship within a pottery tradition. In his recent pieces he places the actual found objects, formerly the inspiration for new work, into tinted, shiny, seductive landscapes or on immaculately executed bases. The figures are always alone in their non-communicating musings or prancings; even when they are grouped each has an individual base.

In one piece, Slee has made an idyllic landscape (*see above*) for the manufactured boy with the red ball to play in; as he stands in the glowing yellow field we

Richard Slee *Boy in Field*, ht. 24 cm (9 ½ in.), 1997
PHOTOGRAPH COURTESY OF THE ARTIST

135

are aware of the unsettling world he inhabits. Beyond the security of the sunny slope is a green field which becomes shadier and cooler as it nears a row of trees, but perhaps they are not trees but rather a row of teeth about to snap closed. Cut off by these at one end, and perched above a gouged-out cliff, the boy can go nowhere, he is stranded in his private, brightly coloured world. The surreal undercurrent and menace in the work are compounded by the professionalism of the execution.

The forms are unpredictable and evolve through the flexible way in which Slee works, assembling the piece from components which are already cut and modelled. He uses a white earthenware clay which he mixes himself and fires at 1080°C/1976°F. He sprays on a basic opaque, white maiolica glaze and then a clear one which is coloured with commercial stains and made up in 10 to 12 different shades so that the colour can be closely graded. A final clear glaze is applied to achieve the utmost brilliance and clarity.

In his work Richard Slee transforms the cosy character of mantelpiece ornaments into uneasy, anxious contemporary figures.

Nicholas Pope *The Apostles Speaking in Tongues,* approx. 180–200 cm (70 ¾ –78 ½ in.), 1996–7

Nicholas Pope did not choose to make his sculptural work in clay. It was in wood, stone and lead that he initially gained an international reputation in the mid-1970s. When he became ill in 1982 he was forced to stop work and later it was necessary to use less physically demanding material. He has said: 'I think clay is one of the most expressive materials for making sculpture.' Like the other sculptors who use clay he is alive to its fundamental qualities, its ability to con-

136

Nicholas Pope, *Doubting Thomas with Three of the Multitude,* Thomas: 270 cm (108 in.), 1996–7

vey detail and its transformation when fired, but for him the paramount consideration is the idea and meaning that it conveys, the reason for arriving at the object.

In 1977 there was a sculptural installation of a group of clay figures by Pope exhibited in the Tate Gallery, called *The Apostles Speaking in Tongues of Fire.* It took the form of coiled vessels constructed in two parts, made of brick clay. It consisted of 12 apostle forms, approximately 270 cm (108 in.) tall, accompanied by 21 others representing the multitudes, 180–200 cm (72–80 in.) tall. The apostles were capped by a simple oil lamp backed by a halo of beaten metal, so that when lit the flickering glow was reflected onto the polished metal and thrown through the open halo. This was to illustrate 'the cloven tongues of fire' which sat upon them on the day of Pentecost. Each apostle is identified by his attributes as drawn from the Bible but translated into abstract detail by the artist; for example Matthew the tax collector carries a heavy paunch, Philip is a smooth-shaven Greek, and the two-faced Judas, the nearest apostle in the picture on p.136, is covered in lascivious lips. *Doubting Thomas* stands with three of the multitude *(previous page)* who were 'confounded because every man heard the speech of his own language'. He is covered with blood-sucking appendages 'sucking the blood from Christ like any doubter sucking energy from those who believe' wrote Pope.

These simple hollow vessels, the method of construction undisguised, have become the containers of a deep and mysterious symbolism. They were envisaged by Pope to be experienced as part of an ambitious project which would place them in a chapel with tunnels and chambers lit by the lamps of the apostles and called *The Oratory of Heavenly Space*.

While the forms of Nicholas Pope are not in any sense realistic they carry with them a familiar narrative and some knowledge of the human qualities of the characters.

Deidre McLoughlin *Old Ecstasy*, 62 x 25 x 30 cm (24 x 10 x 12 in.), 1998
PHOTOGRAPH COURTESY OF THE ARTIST

The sculptures of Deidre McLoughlin do not overtly tell a story. She uses clay to make organic forms which she describes as bimorphic, a term often used to describe the work, among others, of Hans Arp and Brancusi, both of whom included carving in marble in their oeuvres. Some of Deidre McLoughlin's

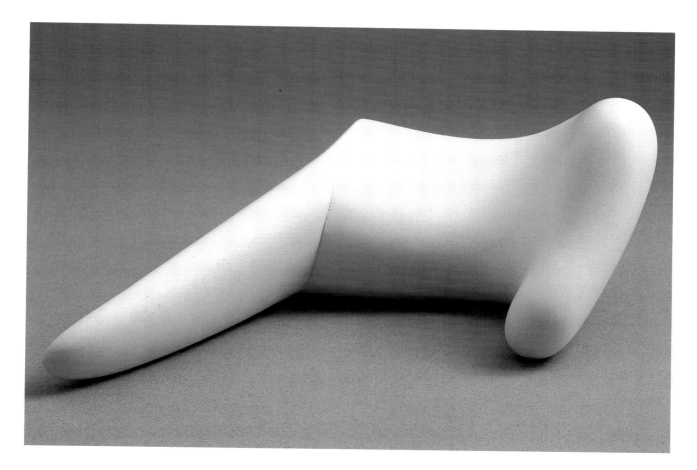

Deidre McLoughlin, *Kuai*, 32 x 24 x 14 cm (13 x 10 x 6 in.), 1996

ceramic forms have the smooth, pared down, precise simplicity of the results of that process.

Her working method is, of course, quite different, starting with the soft, shapeless material of clay. She starts roughly as she goes backwards and forwards on a piece, turning the shape over, supporting it with clay and foam and keeping it smooth enough to see where she is going. Finally a shape comes 'alive' and the tension within it is realised by paring down and grinding back the surface until the flexibility with which she works is totally obliterated. In manipulating the clay she is searching for a form that surprises her and makes 'sense' – a sense which she does not immediately understand. Later, perhaps, she may recognise where a shape has come from as particular resonances with events in her life mingle with other possible meanings.

The titles McLoughlin uses are not directly explanatory; the stoneware sculpture called *Old Ecstasy*, is one of a series *(opposite)* which grew out of the pain she felt for the long years of her father's dying. In abstraction it is a form that curves back on itself, becoming a curved, narrowing, notched, blunt-ended shape. However, there is, as in almost all her work, a subtle allusion to a living being, for it also reads as a sleeping head resting on a pillow. The cavity enclosed by the rounded 'head' allows a shadow to be cast on the cut-out margin to

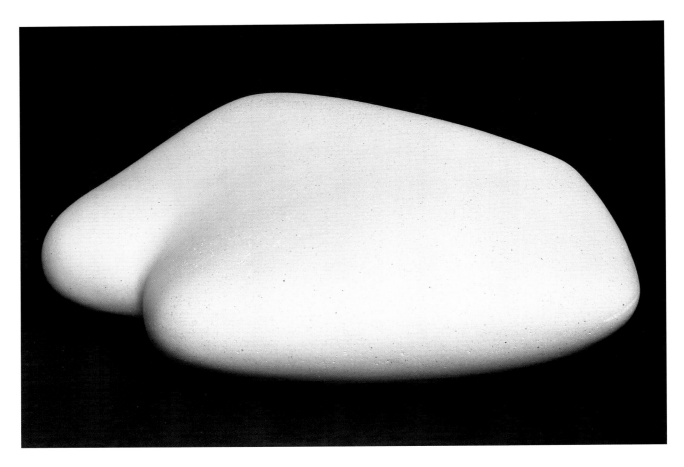

indicate discreetly eyes, nose and mouth. The balance of the piece is finely tuned, as the form lifts from the ground and remains suspended above it.

The smaller, high-fired, polished form (*previous page*) made of T-material is called *Kuai.* It can be read as an abstraction but there is also a strong anatomical suggestiveness about it. Is it a half-reclining figure, with leg outstretched, and a faceless head? Is it a headless torso with arm outstretched and a tilted pelvis? Or is it a three-dimensional shape playing soft, rounded forms against angular ones, curves against lines, shadow against light? It illustrates the artist's search for the tension which lies between rigidity and softness, and the biomorphic balance between the abstract and the figurative.

Kiss-Silence belongs to the same series as *Old Ecstasy.* Is this also a head lying as though on a pillow, or is it the pillow itself? It relates so elusively to both object and living form that the ambiguities and meanings which each of us may sense are best left unsaid, as the artist must have intended.

Final Word

It is hard to decide who or what is the 'hero' or 'heroine' of this book. Is it the artist, the object, the technical innovations, inventions and skills; or is it the history, the geography and archaeology of a diverse range of societies through their ceramic artefacts? Is it the psychological need for human beings to reproduce their circumstances by making images of the thing they know best – themselves, or is it the urge to objectify as a prop to human consciousness, as in the earliest figures? Is it the wish to ignore the finality of death by creating an other-worldly life through ornaments and effigy? Perhaps it is the undefined struggle to identify oneself and the time in which one lives which is central; or maybe it is the desire to decorate and beautify with pictures and symbols, with no other intention but to please. Or is it the unique character of clay itself which has the versatility to interpret a range of styles and ideas while retaining its own identity; a medium used in the only art form – ceramics – to have survived from almost every civilisation from the beginning of time?

Bibliography

General

Flynn, Tom *The Body in Sculpture,* Weidenfeld and Nicolson, 1998

Freestone, Ian and Gaimster, David (Ed.) *Pottery in the Making,* British Museum Press, 1997

McLeod, Malcolm and Mack, John *Ethnic Sculpture,* British Museum Press, 1985

Pioneers of Modern Sculpture, Arts Council of Great Britain, 1973

Read, Herbert *Icon and Idea,* Faber & Faber, London, 1955

Speight, Charlotte, F. *Hands in Clay,* Alfred Publishing Co. U.S.A., 1979

The Burrell Collection, Harper Collins, 1984

Wittowker, Rudolph *Sculpture,* Penguin Books, 1991

Contemporary

Britton, Alison and Margetts, Martina *The Raw and The Cooked* (catalogue of exhibition), The Museum of Modern Art, Oxford, 1993

Rice, Paul and Gowing, Christopher, *British Studio Ceramics,* Barry and Jenkins, London 1989

Watson, Oliver, *British Studio Potters,* Phaidon/Christie's in association with the V & A Museum Publications, London, 1990

Prehistoric

Bahn, Paul G. and Vertut, Jean *Journey Through the Ice Age,* Weidenfeld and Nicolson, 1997

Conkey, M.W., Soffer, O., Stratmann, D., and Jablonski, N., *Beyond Art — Pleistocene Image and Symbol,* Memoir of the Californian Academy of Science, No.23, San Francisco, 1997

Cunliffe, Barry (Ed.) *Oxford Illustrated Prehistory of Europe,* Oxford University Press, 1994

Goodison, Lucy and Morris, Christine, *Ancient Goddesses,* British Museum Press, 1998

Rudgley, Richard *Lost Civilizations of the Stone Age,* Century, London, 1998

Renaissance

Levey, Michael, *Early Renaissance,* Penguin Books, 1991

Olson, Roberta J.M., *Italian Renaissance Sculpture,* Thames and Hudson, 1997

Wilson, Timothy, Maiolica, *Italian Renaissance Ceramics,* Ashmolean Museum, Oxford, 1989

Africa

Barley, Nigel, *Smashing Pots,* British Museum Press, 1994

Eyo, Ekpo and Frank Willett, *Treasures of Ancient Nigeria,* Royal Academy

Fagg, William and Picton, John, *The Potter's Art in Africa,* British Museum Press, 1970

Fagg, William and Plass, Margaret, *African Sculpture,* Studio Vista, 1964

Gillon, Werner, *Collecting African Art,* Studio Vista/Christie's, London, 1979

Phillips, Tom (Ed.), *Africa, The Art of a Continent,* Royal Academy of Arts/Collins, London, 1982

China

Clunes, Craig, *Art in China,* Oxford University Press, 1997

Rawson, Jessica (Ed.), *Mysteries of Ancient China,* British Museum Press, 1996

Tianchou, Fu (Ed.), *The Underground Terracotta Army of Emperor Qin Shi Huan,* New World Press, Beijing

Treager, Mary, *Chinese Art,* Thames and Hudson, (revised edition) 1997

Vainker, S.J., *Chinese Pottery and Porcelain,* British Museum Press, 1995

Watson, William, *The Genius of China,* Times Newspapers Ltd., 1973

Cyprus

Cook, B.F. (Ed.), *Cypriot Art in the British Museum,* British Museum Ltd., 1979

Morris, Desmond, *The Art of Ancient Cyprus,* Phaidon Press, Oxford, 1985

Tatton-Brown, Veronica, *Ancient Cyprus,* British Museum Press, 1997

Egypt

Allen, James W., *Islamic Ceramics,* Ashmolean Museum, Oxford, 1991

Bourriau, Janine *Pottery From the Nile Valley Before the Arab Conquest,* Fitzwilliam Museum, Cambridge, 1981

Caubet, Annie and Pouysseger, Patrick, *The Ancient Near East,* Editions Pierre Terrail, Paris, 1997

Moorey, P.R.S., *Ancient Egypt,* Ashmolean Museum, Oxford, 1983

Moorey, P.R.S., *Ancient Iran,* Ashmolean Museum, Oxford, 1975

Moorey, P.R.S., *Ancient Iraq, Assyria and Babylonia,* Ashmolean Museum, Oxford, 1976

Moorey, P.R.S., *The Ancient Near East,* Ashmolean Museum, Oxford, 1987

Etruria

McNamara, Ellen, *The Etruscans,* B.M. publications, 1990

Strong, Donald, *The Early Etruscans,* Evans Brothers Ltd., London, 1968

European

Atterbury, Paul J., *European Pottery and Porcelain*, Mayflower Books, U.S.A., 1991

Champigneule, Bernard, *Rodin*, Thames and Hudson, 1967

Hook, Moira and McGregor, Arthur, *Medieval England,* British Museum Press, 1991

McCully, Marilyn, *Picasso, Painter and Sculptor in Clay*, Royal Academy of Arts, 1998

Picasso Sculpture, Arts Council of Great Britain, 1967

Ramie, Georges, *Ceramics of Picasso*, Ediciones Poligrafa, Barcelona, 1967

Greece

Boardman, John, *Greek Art*, Thames and Hudson, 1985

Brown, Ann, *Arthur Evans and the Palace of Minos*, Ashmolean Museum, Oxford, 1983

Hanfmann, George M.A., *Classical Sculpture*, Michael Joseph, London, 1967

Vickers, Michael, *Ancient Greek Pottery*, Ashmolean Museum, Oxford, 1999

Vafopoulou-Richardson, C.E., *Greek Terracottas*, Ashmolean Museum, Oxford, 1981

India

Harle, J.C. and Topsfield, Andrew, *Indian Art in the Ashmolean Museum*, Ashmolean Museum, Oxford, 1987

Michell, George (Ed.), *In the Image of Man*, Arts Council of Great Britain, 1982

South America

Bankes, George, *Moche Pottery from Peru*, B.M. Publications, 1990

Pasztory, Esther, *Pre-Columbian Art*, Weidenfeld and Nicolson, 1998

Ryan, Marianne (Ed.), *The Art of Ancient Mexico*, South Bank Centre, London, Olivetti/Electa, 1992

Wutheneu, Alexander von, *Pre-Columbian Terracottas*, Methuen, London, 1965

Journals

Crafts, Crafts Council, London

Ceramic Review, Ceramic Review Publishing Ltd., London

Acknowledgements

I am grateful to the many museums and institutions, credited within these pages, which have kindly supplied photographs. I am particularly indebted to the generous help of the Ashmolean Museum, University of Oxford.

The contemporary ceramic artists were agreeably willing to furnish me with images and information; it has been a pleasure and privilege to talk with them about their work.

There are other individuals who deserve acknowledgement, and they include:
Sheila Paine, who photographed William Newland's work especially for this book; Patricia May, co-author with Maragaret Tuckson, of *The Traditional Pottery of Papua New Guinea* (Bay Books Publishing Company, 1983), who allowed me to use the photograph of the cult pot in chapter 3; Su Lapasco Washington, who lent me photographs of her late husband's pots; Professor R. Marian Hicks O.B.E., who provided me with information about the underground Terracotta Army of Emperor Qin Shi Huang; Wanda Morton, who translated information from the German concerning the Mycenaeon Goddess in Chapter 1; Dr. Peter Leggate, my neighbour, who came to my aid on those occasions when my word-processor decided to act on its own initiative.

Contemporary Applied Arts, London, Flowers East Gallery, London and Peter's Barn Gallery, West Sussex, were all most helpful. I would also like to thank my Commissioning Editor Linda Lambert, for trusting me with this enterprise and my desk editor, Alison Stace for her patience, thoroughness and good-humour.

Finally, I cannot over-estimate the effect of the quiet encouragement and support of my husband, Gwyn Jones.

Index

Page numbers are given for text references, followed by pages with illustrations in italics